עורה הנבל וכנור

*

*Music
Made
in Heaven*

Music

עורה הנבל וכנור

Made

SOME THOUGHTS ON DOVID HAMELECH

in Heaven

AND SEFER TEHILIM

MOSHE M. EISEMANN

Rabbi Moshe M. Eisemann
403 Yeshiva Lane, Apt. 1B
Baltimore, MD 21208
(410) 484-7396

www.kishinievyeshiva.org

Designed by Misha Beletsky

Edited by Sara Eisemann

Cover photograph copyright © Neil Folberg, 2000; www.visiongallery.com

This book was set in Adobe Brioso Pro and Narkiss Classic MFO

ISBN-10: 0-9769161-9-3
ISBN-13: 987-0-9769161-9-2

10   9   8   7   6   5   4   3   2   1

DISTRIBUTED BY:
Feldheim Publishers
POB 35002, Jerusalem, Israel 91350
200 Airport Executive Park, Nanuet, NY 10954
www.feldheim.com

Printed in the USA

CONTENTS

RABBI AHARON FELDMAN

בס"ד

ROSH HAYESHIVA

NER ISRAEL RABBINICAL COLLEGE

STUDY: 400 MT. WILSON LANE (410) 484-7200

RESIDENCE: 409 YESHIVA LANE (410) 653-9433

FAX (410) 484-3060

BALTIMORE, MARYLAND 21208

פורים דמוקפין תשס"ז

Rabbi Eisemann has deeply influenced the students at Ner Yisroel with his classes for over thirty years. It is therefore a matter of great joy for me to learn that he is now disseminating his teachings in book form where they will be available to the general public.

From the essays I have seen it is clear that they are inspiring and incisive in their analysis of their respective topics, as well as beautifully presented through elegant and masterful writing.

It is my hope that this book will be well received by all lovers of Torah learning and that it will be given all the recognition which it truly deserves.

With respects,

Aharon Feldman
Rosh Yeshivas Ner Yisroel
Baltimore, MD

דוד מלך ישראל חי וקים

Of Dovid it is said, כירח יכון עולם ועד בשחק נאמן סלה, As the moon, is established for ever, an enduring witness in the sky. (Tehilim 89:38). Dovid is said to be like the moon. Even though the course of Dovid's life would be a process of constant change as is the moon's; even though, like the moon, he might occasionally even seem to disappear from sight, Dovid, moon-like, shall live and endure for all time.

(Samson Raphael Hirsch, *The Hirsch Siddur*)

I am writing this preface as I am getting ready to send the final batch of materials to the typesetter. I have lived with this book for about a year and can confirm the observation of one of the *chachmei umos haolam* that parting is a sweet sorrow. In this case it is a "sorrow" because I am acutely aware of the book's inadequacies—there is not a single page that could not benefit from rethinking, rewriting and, above all, erasures. Of course that has all been done, but it is never enough. The sweetness is also a player here, because there are parts of the book about which I feel a cautious satisfaction. There are many things that I have learned while I was working on these essays and some of that learning has translated into insights which, so I feel, have some merit.

I started to write this book without any clear vision of where and how it would end. I am sure that everyone who picks it up to read, will realize that it is impossible to even approach exhaustiveness concerning even one incident in Dovid HaMelech's holy life. All along it was a matter of taking a few *pesukim* here and there and attempting to win some insight into this or that detail. I started at a point which seemed particularly relevant to me—the relationship between Dovid HaMelech and *Kiddush HaChodesh*—and hoped that as I wrote, the issues themselves would point me in directions which might help me locate and develop the ideas which were germinating in my mind. That is how the book was written and I offer it to the reader in the hope that he or she will judge me and it kindly and use it as a springboard for further thought and further fruitful development.

Before I decided to move from writing to publication, I asked a respected colleague to read it through and point out its most egregious faults to me. As he has done in the past he took his mandate seriously and made extremely valuable comments. One of these was that, too often, I make certain assumptions for which there is no source in TaNaCh or in Chazal. He was kind enough to point out the specific places which disturbed him. I studied each instance carefully and, I suppose inevitably—*midos* being what they are—decided to stick with what I had written. I felt that the assumptions which I made lay sufficiently near the surface of material that does exist, to justify them.

In the course of our discussion he pointed out to me the responsibility which an author has to his readers. They trust him not to deceive them, and want to feel that in a book such as this they can take what is given as tested and appropriate. I took what he said to heart and provide an endnote at each of the locations to which he objected, to point out that, at that particular juncture, the reader should assume an amber flashing light and proceed with caution.

I thank him and all of you for your interest.

Adding Sweetness to Israel's Songs

*T*his book is about Sefer Tehilim. It is about Sefer Tehilim, even though Sefer Tehilim will hardly be mentioned. The Sefer that will be mentioned in almost every chapter and that will provide the many passages we will study in great depth is Sefer Shmuel. Now I know that this does not make much sense to you, dear reader, and it is hard to explain without going into the kind of detail that does not belong in a brief introductory chapter. I will give you just a short paragraph here, and for the rest I ask you to trust me that, as you make your way through *Music Made in Heaven*, everything will turn out all right.

My goal is to answer a question that seems to me to be very compelling. It is this. Why does Sefer Shmuel not quote any of the Tehilim that, as their introductory verse often testifies, were said in the context of events very carefully spelled out in Sefer Shmuel? Telling the story and leaving out the fact that it served Dovid as inspiration for one of his immortal compositions is giving a very truncated account. An incomplete picture lacks certain dimensions of the truth. A truth that is not rounded off is a half-truth. How can Sefer Shmuel be satisfied with teaching us half-truths?

I will propose my answer to this question in the final chapter of *Music Made in Heaven*. It will be built around an assumption that I will make concerning the respective characters of Sefer Shmuel and Sefer Tehilim. Sefer Shmuel, in its own terms, will be shown to be complete and lacking nothing. I will argue that Sefer Shmuel and Sefer Tehilim occupy two entirely different worlds. The points of reference of the one are not those of the other. A chapter of Tehilim in the narrative parts of Shmuel would be like a total stranger at a wedding—he just somehow does not seem to fit in.

It is in this sense that, as I said above, *Music Made in Heaven* is about Sefer Tehilim, although Sefer Tehilim is hardly mentioned. We will reach certain conclusions about the nature of Sefer Shmuel. Once we have established that, we will suggest that, by its own nature, Sefer Tehilim has no place there. We will arrive at conclusions about Sefer Tehilim that grow out of its incompatibility with Sefer Shmuel.

I hope this short explanation has not discouraged you from reading on. As I said before, by the time you get to the final chapter, all will be clear.

Since Sefer Tehilim really comes up short in this book, I want to use the rest of this introduction to share some thoughts with you about Dovid in his capacity as the sweet singer of Israel's songs (II Shmuel 23:1).

* * * * * * * * * * * *

עורה כבודי
עורה הנבל וכנור
אעירה שחר

*

Awaken o my soul
Awaken o harp and lyre
I wish to arouse the very dawn
(Tehilim 57:9)

* * * * * * * * * * * *

At II Shmuel 23:1 Dovid introduces himself as the *one who lends sweetness to Israel's songs*. The compositions that make up Sefer Tehilim apparently have a very special sweetness to them. Let us see whether we can trace the source of this unusual characterization.

רב אשי אמר עד חצות לילה היה עוסק בדברי תורה מכאן ואילך בשירות
ותשבחות.
Rav Ashi taught, "Until midnight Dovid would immerse himself in Torah studies. From midnight onwards he busied himself with songs and praises."
(Berachos 3b)

Dovid slept very little. He seems to have taken occasional catnaps during the day—never more than sixty breaths at a time—but that would end with nightfall. The night was to be dedicated to Torah and Tehilim. The change from the one to the other took place at midnight, as the Gemara quoted above makes clear.

The Gemara wonders how Dovid would know that midnight had arrived and that it was time to enter the world of song. Here is the answer:

דוד סימנא הוה ליה דאמר רב אחא בר ביזנא אמר רבי שמעון חסידא כנור היה תלוי למעלה ממטתו של דוד וכיון שהגיע חצות לילה בא רוח צפונית ונושבת בו ומנגן מאליו מיד היה עומד ועוסק בתורה עד שעלה עמוד השחר.

Dovid was always able to tell when it was midnight...there was a harp suspended above his bed and when midnight arrived a north wind would stimulate the harp to play by itself. Upon hearing its music Dovid would immediately rise and busy himself with Torah until day would break.[1]

Most of us have heard many times about this harp that was suspended above Dovid's bed. Until I happened across it recently, I do not recall ever asking myself why this was significant. I can't believe that it was simply an old-fashioned alarm clock installed to alert Dovid that the exact moment of midnight had come. It seems so unlikely that it was of paramount importance that Dovid should switch from learning to *songs and praises* at an exact moment. Why would a few minutes earlier or later have made such a difference?

When this question struck me, it occurred to me that it might be a good idea to look into Dovid's skill as a musician. I began wondering why the Tehilim needed to be set to music. We know none of the original tunes that Dovid composed and in spite of that we are greatly inspired by the words standing on their own. So the music seems to be a luxury with which we can dispense. Why were Tehilim set to music?

And yet, the case can be made that music on its own, even when not set to words, is perhaps the choicest form of praising the Ribono shel Olam. I have heard the point made by the late Rav Joseph B. Soloveichik that it is remarkable that Tehilim 150, the very last *mizmor* in Sefer Tehilim, appears to eschew words completely. We are called upon to praise God with all manner of instruments, with not even a hint that these should accompany some verbal composition. It makes a strange ending indeed to a book that records 149 poems. Rav Soloveichik suggested that this *mizmor* articulated Dovid's sense that *to You silence is the greatest praise;*[2] that the most inspired words must inevitably fall short of what really needs to be said. The less said, the better; the more inspired music we can draw from our instruments, the more untainted will our praises be.

I decided to check into what TaNaCh had to say about Dovid the musician as opposed to Dovid the author of Tehilim. The place to look, so it seemed to me, was back at the very beginning, when Shaul's advisers suggested that Dovid's music might help the king out of his depression. I looked at that *parashah* and was struck by a peculiarity. Here are two of the relevant *p'sukim* from I Shmuel 16:16 and 23.

טו. ...יבקשו איש ידע מנגן בכנור והיה בהיות עליך רוח אלהים רעה ונגן בידו וטוב לך.

כג. והיה בהיות רוח אלהים אל שאול ולקח דוד את הכנור ונגן בידו ורוח לשאול וטוב לו וסרה מעליו רוח הרעה.

16. ...Let them look for a man who is able to play music on a harp and it will be when you will suffer from an evil spirit from God, he will be able to play *with his hands* and you will feel better.

23. It came about that whenever the spirit of God came upon Shaul, Dovid would take the harp and play *with his hands* and the spirit of Shaul improved and the evil spirit would leave him.

Why in these two verses is there a stress upon the fact that Dovid would play *with his hands*? It cannot be that this is just a manner of speaking, since, when the servants suggested that a musician be found, they said simply, *a man who is able to play music on the harp.* They said nothing of the fact that the musician would be using his hands. Why then make an issue of it when it came to Dovid?

Let us now return to the question of the harp hanging over Dovid's bed. We wondered what might have been the point of such an arrangement.

I cannot know what music the north wind plucked from that famous harp nor have I any idea how it sounded. However, clearly it was celestial music, unlike any composed by man. I believe that Dovid waited until midnight to switch from Torah learning to composing his Tehilim because he waited to be inspired by the heavenly music he would hear as the north wind wrought its magic.

If we are on the right track, then we have a ready explanation for the fact that Shaul's advisers made an issue out of the fact that Dovid would be playing his harp *with his hands*. They had heard Dovid play and they knew that his music was different from any other they had ever heard. Dovid had eavesdropped on the music of the angels—every night his trusted harp had marked midnight with music sent from heaven. Shaul's advisers could not contain their wonder that human hands could create such music. It is this that they stressed to Shaul.

At the beginning of this section we wondered whether we could have some idea of the sweetness with which Dovid was able to imbue Israel's songs. What was it that lent Tehilim their magic? I think we have the answer. In his Tehilim, with his harp, Dovid was able to bring a little piece of heaven down to us.[3]

ONE

Jumping for Salvation

*I*t was in the waning years of the Evil Empire. Moscow was still very much Moscow. We were watched and we were followed. For the KGB ruffians who were assigned to us, we were the enemy. True, learning with the *Asirei Tzion* was necessary and gratifying, but there were still times when we felt worn down. The unrelieved drabness that colored everything a dirty gray seemed symbolic of the hopeless future that appeared to mock our newfound Russian friends.

It was a *Motzoei Shabbos* on a freezing winter night. It was time for *Kidush Levanah* and we decided, in spite of the risks, to stand outside and do what we needed to do. As ugly and depressing as the surroundings were, so glorious and cleansing was the star-spangled sky. The moon, bright and friendly, bid us welcome. It suddenly struck me that this was the very same moon I knew so well from back on Yeshiva Lane in Baltimore. It was great to see a familiar face. I fantasized that at this very moment my wife and children might be looking at it over there. (Alright, so I forgot the seven-hour time difference.) For a moment the thousands of miles between us seemed to melt away. It was like a little bit of home, and that was enough for me.

We Jews are a moon-people. The sun seems to scare us; it is too brash for our taste. Often too bright, often too hot, it is just too intrusive. Koheles does not tire of telling us of all the terrible things that can happen when life is lived "beneath the sun." We find the moon much more congenial. We like its modesty as, sliver by sliver, it shyly approaches the sun. We like its courage when, never fazed by having faded into nothingness, it returns undaunted and works hard, night by night, to make it back to the glory of its fullness.

Here is what Ramo has to say in Hilchos Birkas HaLevanah (426:2):

ונוהגין לומר דוד מלך ישראל חי וקיים שמלכותו נמשל ללבנה ועתיד
להתחדש כמותה וכנסת ישראל תחזור להתדבק בבעלה שהוא הקב"ה

דוגמת הלבנה המתחדשת עם החמה שנאמר שמש ומגן ה' ולכך עושין
שמחות ורקודין בקידוש החדש דוגמת שמחת נשואין.

During the monthly Moon Blessing it is customary to
say the sentence, "Dovid, King of Israel, lives and endures." We do this, because his kingship is compared to
the moon, and will one day be renewed just as the moon
is always renewed. Moreover, the moon fills us with
confidence. Its determination to renew its contact with
the sun reminds us of a wife who has become estranged
from her husband, but in the end makes her way back to
him.... This association with renewed marital bliss calls
us to dance at Kidush HaChodesh, just as one does at a
wedding.

I think that there is something very beautiful and moving
about these dances. Month after month we go at it, confident
that even if the wedding date may not yet have been fixed, the
choson must already be on the way.

There is another little ceremony that we perform at the
Birchas HaLevanah, one which we ought to contemplate as
we get ready to think about Dovid HaMelech, the Melech
HaMoshiach.

ורוקד ג' פעמים כנגדה ואומר כשם שאני רוקד כו' ואומר תפול עליהם וגו'
ולמפרע כאבן ידמו כו' ג' פעמים.

A person engaged in Birkas HaLevanah takes three
dance steps propelling him upward toward the moon
and says, "Just as I am leaping towards you and can never
hope to touch you, so should my enemies be unable to
touch me with the intention of harming me." He then
continues with a prayer beginning with the words, "May
fear and terror strike my enemies...," which he repeats
three times.

As I keep looking at what I have just written, I find it hard to
contain myself at the wonder of it all. How long has it been
since the Ramo recorded these unbelievable words? How
many centuries before he wrote it was the custom already in

use?[1] So many months; so many jumps. Apparently the truth has not yet sunk in. We are all still jumping, reaching for the unreachable. We keep hoping. Perhaps one day, against all that experience has taught us, we will reach that which will have become the reachable.

What does all this say about us?

Who was the first person who jumped that jump? Of course we cannot know. But somehow, somewhere, someone felt the need to convey his hopes and dreams to the Ribono shel Olam. "Look," he was saying, "see how much we long to touch the moon, symbol of Dovid HaMelech's kingship, and, through it, to draw closer to Dovid HaMelech himself. Oh I know it doesn't really make sense. I know that my feet are firmly anchored down here, wholly removed from the world of the spheres. But then how much sense does it make for us, after so many disappointments, so many tears, to keep on hoping, 'Every day I long fiercely that he should come!'[2] I refuse to let reality cow me into passivity. If, in practical terms, my expectations are small, my dreams touch infinity."

And, perhaps as he was saying all this to himself, or better still, to the Ribono shel Olam within himself, another thought crossed his mind. "It is true that though my soul is flying high, my feet are feet of clay. But, real reality deals with souls and not with feet. Perhaps my longings will define me more accurately than does gravity. O Ribono shel Olam, please grant that although these silly little jumps will not bring me closer to the moon, they will nevertheless put me beyond the reach of my enemies. I may not have reached the sky but, just a little bit, I have left the earth behind. It is the earth that is my enemy's domain. In leaving that earth behind me, grant that I will have left the ambit of their clutches."

There is something very defining about Jewish hope for Moshiach. Let us take a look at Rambam Hilchos Melachim 11:1.

המלך המשיח עתיד לעמוד ולהחזיר מלכות דוד ליושנה לממשלה הראשונה ובונה המקדש ומקבץ נדחי ישראל וחוזרין כל המשפטים בימיו כשהיו מקודם מקריבין קרבנות ועושין שמטין ויובלות ככל מצותה

האמורה בתורה וכל מי שאינו מאמין בו או מי שאינו מחכה לביאתו לא
בשאר נביאים בלבד הוא כופר אלא בתורה ובמשה רבינו.

The Melech HaMoshiach will one day arise and reestablish Dovid's Kingship to its original royal prerogative. He will rebuild the Beis HaMikdash and bring back all the exiles of Israel....Whoever does not believe in him or *who does not eagerly anticipate his coming* denies not only all the prophetic writings but also Moshe Rabbeinu's Torah.

Now, it is noteworthy that Rambam himself, in Hilchos Teshuvah 3:9, defines very clearly who can be deemed to have denied Moshe Rabbeinu's Torah.[3] They are: a.) one who claims that there is no Torah given by the Ribono shel Olam; b.) one who denies any of the interpretations of the written Torah that are authenticated by tradition; or c.) one who claims that the laws the Ribono shel Olam commanded us in the Torah have no validity any more because they have been changed to other laws.

Clearly, one who does not *eagerly anticipate his coming* does not fall into any of these categories. Why, then, would Rambam in Hilchos Melachim accuse him of being in denial of Moshe Rabbeinu's Torah?

As far as I can see, the only possible explanation must lie in the unique magic that the anticipation of a Messianic future would exercise upon a Jew who truly believes that it will inevitably come about. Now the Rambam from Hilchos Melachim that we quoted above asserts that the Torah contains a number of passages that make it absolutely clear that there will be an ultimate redemption. Here is a quote and a translation of the beginning of this passage:

שהרי התורה העידה עליו שנאמר ושב ה' אלהיך את שבותך ורחמך ושב
וקבצך וגו' אם יהיה נדחך בקצה השמים וגו' והביאך ה' ואלו הדברים
המפורשים בתורה הם כוללים כל הדברים שנאמרו על ידי כל הנביאים.

For the Torah testifies that a Moshiach will come, as it is written (Devarim 30:3), *HaShem your God will bring back those of you who had been taken captive and will have mercy upon you, once more He will gather you from among the*

nations....Even if your exiles will have been scattered to the
very ends of the heavens, HaShem your God will gather you in
from there and bring you back. Now, all these descriptions
that are quite plainly written in the Torah, really cover
everything that was foreseen by the later prophets.

Taken together with what we maintained in the previous
paragraph, it can be asserted unequivocally that only one who
denies the Torah would fail to *eagerly anticipate his coming.*
In the words of the late, great Rav Hutner, an authentic Jew
has a *bulimus*, a ravenous hunger that may not be denied,[4] for
Messianic redemption.

And so, we Yidden continue to feel blessed every month
when the new moon once more peeks out at us. We see in
this monthly drama an earnest of our own renewal and, un-
deterred by centuries of unrealized hope, we dance with joy
and trust, anticipating, as we have done for millennia, that the
choson is on his way, is, in fact, just around the corner.

As always, the centerpiece of our celebration continues
to be:

דוד מלך ישראל חי וקים

*

Dovid, King of Israel, lives and endures

TWO

Gad, the Precursor of Eliyahu Hanavi

ould you like to give yourself a little test? Jot down everything you know about the tribe of Gad, Yaakov Avinu's seventh son. I know that if I had been challenged to do that before I thought things through in preparation for this chapter, I would have been hard put to fill up more than a quarter of a page. Of course you may wonder why, in writing a book about Dovid HaMelech, the Melech HaMoshiach, I would want to think so much about Gad. Well, *you* would be right to wonder, but *I* was right to think. By the end of this chapter, I think you might agree.

Let us begin with Gad and Reuven's radical[1] request that Moshe Rabbeinu grant them permission to settle on the eastern bank of the Yarden (BeMidbar 32). Life in those exposed areas, particularly for sheep ranchers, would be difficult. They would be subject to the attacks of marauders much more than would those of their brothers who would have settled in Eretz Yisrael proper. The tribe of Gad, fierce fighters all (see Devarim 33:20), was less intimidated at this prospect than was the tribe of Reuven. They felt that they were well equipped to handle any eventuality, and it was they, not Reuven, who initiated the request (Ramban 32:2).

On the surface, the story, as told in BeMidbar, seems simple enough. The needs of these two tribes were determined by the huge flocks they owned. They required vast grazing lands; the east bank was able to provide that, so why not make their homes there?

However, this straightforward account of what happened takes on a very different coloration in Moshe Rabbeinu's blessing addressed to Shevet Gad (Devarim 33:21).

וירא ראשית לו כי שם חלקת מחקק ספון ויתא ראשי עם צדקת יהוה עשה ומשפטיו עם ישראל.

The translation should be given at this point, but we are not yet quite ready. The language is poetic, the precise meaning

11

obscure. That goes for even the first phrase, which is relatively clear, although not all the commentators are of one mind. Concerning the second half of the sentence, there is no consensus at all. We will have to make a choice from among an unusually rich range of offerings

Rashi will serve as our guide for the first half of the verse.

[Gad] selected the very first available[2] [inheritance] because it was there that the grave[3] of the lawgiver lay concealed.

The "lawgiver" in this context is Moshe Rabbeinu. His grave is "concealed" since its location was known to no man. It lies somewhere in Gad's portion of the land and played a significant role in Gad's decision to settle there.

This verse paints a very different picture from the one that emerges from the BeMidbar account. There, the ready availability of the vast pastures of the east bank was the only consideration. No other advantages were mooted. Indeed, why would they have been? So we have a problem to solve: what could Moshe Rabbeinu possibly have meant when he injected this apparently extraneous idea into the story?

The answer must be, of course, that it is not extraneous at all. It seems to me that we must understand the phrase as Moshe Rabbeinu's commentary to the account in Matos. It certainly needed a commentary. The other tribes must have looked askance at Gad and Reuven's decision to remain in Ever HaYarden. It must have appeared to them as an inexcusable distortion of values. The dreams that had been nurtured during the forty years of desert wandering had always been focused, for very good reasons, on the land that lay to the west of the Yarden.[4] Gad's decision must have been viewed as a betrayal of all the hopes that had animated the people from the moment they had left Egypt.

It is quite possible that, in its own way, it had the same potential of wakening suspicions as had the altar that the two and a half tribes were to build years later, as discussed in endnote 2. At the very least it seemed to portend the beginnings of a weakening of the ties which bound the twelve tribes into an indivisible whole.

Moshe Rabbeinu used the occasion of his farewell address to set the record straight. It is true that Gad was motivated by the need to assure sufficient pasture for his flocks. However, even the most logical argument must founder if necessary conditions for its implementation are missing. Obviously, if the most exquisitely luscious grazing grounds would have been available far away from Eretz Yisrael, Gad would not even have considered them. But Ever HaYarden was not far away. It could, in fact, be made a part of Eretz Yisrael if Moshe Rabbeinu would be willing to have it settled. The presence, albeit a presence shrouded in mystery, of Moshe Rabbeinu's grave clinched the matter for him. The problems with which he might be faced by living on the east bank held no terrors for him. Moshe Rabbeinu would be there to watch over him.

But, it does not end there. There is more, much more. Let us now turn to the second half of the sentence and see what insights it can yield.

What are we to make of *tzidkas HaShem asah*? A literal translation would read, *he did the charity of God*. That does not convey much to us. Before we attempt to understand what is meant, we will have to make a decision about the pronoun *he*. Does it refer to Gad whom Moshe Rabbeinu is addressing in this phrase, or does it go back to the *mechokek* (Moshe Rabbeinu) who was mentioned earlier? The syntax could yield either interpretation, so we will follow Rashi who has it refer to Gad.[5]

Ha'amek Davar offers an interpretation that, when we think about it, offers a gateway to a profound understanding of Gad and his place among the twelve tribes. He believes that the phrase is meant to convey that Gad performed an act of charity *to* God. The Ribono shel Olam would not have been happy if Moshe Rabbeinu had had his way and would have left the eastern bank of the Yarden uninhabited. The Ribono shel Olam would not have wanted any land that could potentially have carried the sanctity of Eretz Yisrael to be left to lie desolate. It was an act of charity on Gad's part to shoulder the risks and difficulties to which he would expose himself by living in the less protected areas in the east, in order to give the Ribono shel Olam the satisfaction of seeing His entire land inhabited by His beloved people.

That given, we have now met Gad as one for whom it is important to do a kindness to the Ribono shel Olam. Our next question should be whether there is anything that we know about Gad that would provide us with a clue as to why just he, from among all the *shevatim*, was particularly endowed with this characteristic. It turns out that indeed there is. To find what we are seeking, we go back to the sequence in which Yaakov Avinu's children were born. Leah bore four sons, Reuven, Shimon, Levi, and Yehudah, in succession. Then Rachel gave her maid-servant, Bilhah, to Yaakov and Bilhah bore Dan and Naftali. After that, Leah gave her maid-servant Zilpah to Yaakov and Zilpah bore Gad and Osher. Following that, Leah herself bore Yissachar and Zevulun.

Bereishis 30:18 explains why Leah named her son Yissachar. The name derives from the root word *schar*, which means "reward." Leah was sure that she had been gifted with this fifth son as a reward for her selflessness in permitting her husband to marry Zilpah. In contrast to Rachel, who had, so to speak, been forced by her barrenness to take such a radical path, Leah, the proud mother of four sons, had no need to make this sacrifice. She took this painful step purely as an act of kindness to her husband.[6] That kindness, she felt, was now being acknowledged through the gift of a fifth son (Chizkuni, there).[7]

Gad, then, was born of a match that had been brought about directly by a gesture of goodness on the grandest of grand scales. Small wonder, then, that he had been endowed with the same characteristic. Leah had shown a loving understanding for her husband's needs. Shevet Gad would do no less for the Ribono shel Olam Himself.

And, let us note, for the Ribono shel Olam's children. In the first place, by electing to remain on the exposed eastern bank, the tribe shouldered the burden of absorbing the brunt of any attack by Israel's malevolent neighbors to the east. Then there was more, much more. A careful reading of BeMidbar 32:20–22 yields that Moshe Rabbeinu, as a condition to granting their request, demanded that they cross the Yarden together with the rest of the people, take part in the fighting that would surely ensue, and remain there until the enemy had been conquered. That would have obligated them to remain away from home for seven years (Zevachim 118b). In reality, they remained in Eretz Yisrael proper for double that time, a full fourteen years, waiting out not only the conquest to be completed but also for the division of the land.[8]

It is worthwhile to quote a passage from Michtav Mei-Eliyahu (volume 2, page 259), in which he extols the unusual sensitivity that Reuven[9] and Gad displayed in this matter. Seven years, after all, is no small matter. Here is a paraphrase of what Rav Dessler writes:

> [They viewed the entire incident as an opportunity to serve the Ribono shel Olam heroically.] They fulfilled the task that their sense of responsibility had imposed upon them to a point at which they reached the very peak of kindness and consideration. They determined not to return to their homes until the division of the land had been completed—a period of seven long years. They did not wish to have their own lives in order as long as even one of their brethren had not yet attained an equivalent level of comfort.

We have come to a point in this essay at which we are ready to offer the perplexed reader an explanation. What does this analysis of Shevet Gad's role in Jewish history have to do with a book that purports to be about Dovid HaMelech?

We will fast-forward to the time when Dovid was a fugitive from Shaul's anger. He knew that if he remained in Eretz Yisrael it would be only a matter of time until he was found. He fled the land and found shelter with the Philistine Achish, king of Gath. He settled in a town called Tziglag. At first he used this town as a base from which he went marauding against Israel's enemies. At a later date, Achish forced him to desist from these activities, and from then on he remained permanently in Tziglag. (For details see I Shmuel, chapter 26 and onward).

Dovid's prospects of ever occupying the throne must have seemed, at that time, dim indeed. He was an outcast, unable to find a single corner in Eretz Yisrael that would have welcomed him. Who, under such circumstances, would have elected to join him? However, against all expectations, groups of seasoned soldiers from all the tribes began to find their way to him. There seems to have been an irresistible magnetism that drew sensitive people to God's anointed.

It is an exciting story, one that tells of the intuitive attraction that *yidden* feel toward Dovid Melech Yisrael. It makes us feel good; it stokes the fires of our own longing for his return. The Chronicler (I Divrei HaYamim, chapter 12), recognizing the festive undertone that accompanies this ingathering, fits his language to the occasion by using a heightened prose, one that intimates that something very special is happening. However, nothing in that chapter even approaches the sense of drama with which he introduces the Gadites who joined Dovid at Tziglag.

> Of the Gadites, there withdrew to follow Dovid to the wilderness stronghold, valiant men, fighters fit for battle, armed with shield and spear. Faces like those of a lion, swift as gazelles upon the mountains....The least among them was equal to a hundred, the greatest to a thousand....These were the ones who crossed the Yarden in the first month, when it was at its crest, and they put the lowlanders to flight.
>
> (I Divrei HaYamim 12:9–16)

The Vilna Gaon goes so far as to suggest that their gazelle-like speed was such that when they *crossed the Yarden,* they actually walked upon the water.

What was it that energized these mighty warriors? What inner flame lent a lion's glow to their faces? What sped their feet across the mountains and upon the waters?

It seems to me that we can best understand all this according to the opinion (recorded in Bereishis Rabba 71:9 and sundry midrashim) that Eliyahu HaNavi is descended from Gad. The midrashim do not offer any explanations for either the fact of this familial relationship or for its significance. They simply provide the proof text upon which they base their assertion. We have spent so much effort in this essay trying to understand Gad and his role in our history, that we should make some attempt to understand this final detail.

I suggest that Eliyahu HaNavi's aptness for the task of announcing the coming of Moshiach is firmly bound to the two qualities that we have found to constitute the very essence of Gad's nature. You cannot accompany Klal Yisrael through the fearsome valleys of its exile without caring profoundly for its well-being. You can certainly not hear the footfalls of Moshiach in the clamor and confusion of tumultuous history without being exquisitely attuned to God's dreadful longing to escape the desecration of His name, which is a necessary result of His children's absence from home.[10] Gad who was willing to give up on life in Eretz Yisrael proper and thereby to shoulder the onus of protecting his brothers from attack; Gad who picked up God's craving that the east bank should be imbued with the sanctity of Eretz Yisrael, can bring up an Eliyahu HaNavi among his sons.

I think that we now know enough to explain the special treatment that the Chronicler reserved for the contingent from Gad. The other heroes from the other tribes were sufficiently perceptive to catch a glimpse of Dovid, God's anointed, that lay hidden beneath the outer appearance of the hapless fugitive whom nobody else was willing to credit. There was much to be admired in such perspicacity. Gad, however, was in another league. He saw further, much further. Gad/Eliyahu's vision was not limited to the Dovid of the here and now. It took him down the centuries, and, behold, there was Dovid in the garb of his descendant, the Melech HaMoshiach. That was a different story altogether.

We will devote the rest of this book to see whether we can catch a glimpse of what it is that the Gadites saw.

The Monarchy

*T*he time has come for us to think about the institution of the monarchy. For us who live in twenty-first-century America, the desirability of living under an absolute sovereign, even when his rule is benign, is not self-evident. It is true that we are all acutely and painfully aware of the dark underside of democracy as we experience it, but we also treasure its wonderful gifts. Something tells me that even in our own society, one that happily and with a feeling of privilege subordinates itself to *gedolei Yisrael,* an imposed hegemony would be resisted. Certainly if these *gedolim* would draft our sons to *harness them to their chariots and have them serve as outrunners,* or our daughters to be *cooks and bakers* in their kitchens,[1] our enthusiasm would quickly cool.

Chazal seem to take a very bleak view of the monarchy as it was practiced from the investiture of Shaul as king until its disintegration when the first commonwealth was dissolved. Here is a paraphrase of Devarim Rabbah 5:11:

God said to us, "In these pre-Messianic times you asked that I grant you kings to rule over you. I complied with your request and gave you kings. You soon found out that these caused you untold troubles. There was Shaul whose war cost many lives on Mount Gilbo'a. Dovid brought a plague upon you and Achav, a drought. Tzidkiyahu caused the Beis HaMikdash to be destroyed."

When the Jews realized that the monarchy brought many tragedies in its wake, they all cried out, "We want no kings! We want only the Ribono shel Olam to be our king. For it is written, 'For HaShem is our Judge, HaShem is our lawgiver, HaShem is our king, only He will save us.'"

God heard their cries and promised, "That is precisely what I will do." For it is written, "On that day HaShem will be king over the entire earth."

The general thesis of this midrash can be derived from Yechezkel, chapter 34. There God promises that in the Messianic future He will do away with the monarchy entirely and will Himself rule over His children. So the monarchy did not live up to expectations and the midrash is solidly grounded in TaNaCh. However, it seems deeply shocking that the midrash includes Dovid among the kings whom it excoriates. That certainly seems incongruent with the Dovid whom the Gadites perceived and for whom they crossed the rushing waters.

Let us take a closer look at the Yechezkel passage. We are in for some surprises.

The passage uses lazy, self-serving shepherds who care more for themselves than for their flocks, as a metaphor for the kings.

> Woe unto you, shepherds of Israel…is it right that you eat the fat, that you clothe yourselves in the wool, that you slaughter the choicest, all this while not tending the sheep? The frail you have not strengthened; the ill you have not cured; the broken you have not bandaged; the banished you have not retrieved; the lost you have not sought.…My sheep wander among all the mountains… and have been scattered over the whole earth. No one is interested in their fate.
>
> (Yechezkel 34:2–6)

There is more, much more, all in the same vein. The section is a chilling appraisal of four hundred years of Jewish history, Jewish failure, delivered by Yechezkel on the threshold of the *churban*. No doubt that during this period there were moments of high hopes. It was not all unrelieved darkness. But, taken all together, the verdict must have cut like a lash.

Let us look at the Rambam (Melachim 2:6) to learn from him what the Torah really expects from a king. No doubt it will make us sadder, but it is important that we have some help in appreciating the dimensions of the tragedy.

ויהיה חונן ומרחם לקטנים וגדולים ויצא ויבא בחפציהם ובטובתם ויחוס
על כבוד קטן שבקטנים...לעולם יתנהג בענוה יתירה...ויסבול טרחם
ומשאם ותלונותם וקצפם כאשר ישא האומן את היונק רועה קראו הכתוב
לרעות ביעקב עמו ודרכו של רועה מפורש בקבלה כרועה עדרו ירעה
בזרועו יקבץ טלאים ובחיקו ישא.

Let him be caring and merciful to all of them equally.
Let the attention to their needs fill his time. He should
be sensitive to the feelings of even the least important
among them. Let him be patient and understanding of
their importuning and the burdens that they lay upon
him, their grumblings and their angers, just as a caring nurse will treat the infant in her charge. The Torah
calls him a shepherd. Now shepherds care deeply for
their sheep. They gather them in and carry them in their
arms.

It is sad, is it not?

After castigating the shepherd/kings, the Ribono shel
Olam declares that the time will come when He will dispense
with them and, instead, will Himself look after His sheep: *I
Myself will take care of My sheep, and make sure that I know their
needs* (verse 11). He then continues:

It will be I Who will search for the lamb that has been
lost; I Who will make sure that the one who was driven
away will be restored. I will bind up their broken limbs
and attend to the sick among them. The fat and strong
ones [who tend to push the others around] I will drive
away. The care that I will lavish upon them will be entirely fair (verse 15).

Well and good. It is exactly what we would have expected after the harsh criticism that the Ribono shel Olam had lev-
eled against the kings. The monarchy had turned out to be an
experiment that had failed. It will be eliminated. If we are to
associate this assessment with the description that we quoted
above from the midrash, then all the kings, including even

Dovid, had simply fallen short of the high standards that were demanded if the monarchy were going to work.

How shocking then, to read the following only a few verses later:

והושעתי לצאני ולא תהיינה עוד לבז ושפטתי בין שה לשה. והקמתי עליהם
רעה אחד ורעה אתהן את עבדי דויד הוא ירעה אתם והוא יהיה להן לרעה.
ואני יהוה אהיה להם לאלהים ועבדי דוד נשיא בתוכם אני יהוה דברתי.

I will save My sheep and they will no longer be left as spoil to the marauders. I will establish justice between one sheep and the next. I will appoint one shepherd who will look after them. It will be My servant Dovid. He will look after them and he will be their shepherd. Then I, HaShem, will be their God and My servant Dovid will be a prince among them. I, HaShem, have spoken (verses 22–23).

What can it all mean? Is there not a blatant contradiction here?

We have opened the door a crack. What we suspected at the end of the last chapter appears to be true. A gap is opening between the historical and the messianic Dovid. From now on it is up to us to follow the clues and to develop a thesis. If we do it well we will become wiser and, who knows, perhaps even better Jews. It will be an exciting quest.

FOUR

Shaul's Downfall Is Rooted in His Perfection

*L*et us begin at the beginning. Let us watch Dovid make his entry into Jewish history. It is a dramatic scene, one that will surely remain with us as we become more and more involved in his life and in his and our destiny. Let us, above all, remember that we are learning Kisvei HaKodesh and that the sections of Sefer Shmuel we shall study are the thoughts of the Ribono shel Olam conveyed to us through Shmuel HaNavi's pen. Nothing is trite, nothing superfluous, nothing but that it is designed to form our Jewish thinking, our Jewish living, and our Jewish dreams. Let us then remove the shoes of our ordinariness; the ground that we are about to tread is holy.

I imagine that anyone who learns Sefer Shmuel would wish that Dovid's elevation to the kingship had come about under happier circumstances than those that resulted from the tragic degeneration of Shaul. That, however, is a story that deserves its own treatment. Our discussion must begin after Shaul had been rejected so that we are spared the sorrow of having to analyze the fall of that great tzadik.

We will begin in I Shmuel, chapter 16, the moment when Shmuel appears in Yishai's home. It was an auspicious moment. Shmuel knew that he was about to play the decisive role in bringing the kingship to its permanent home. Shaul was a Binyominite, and it was clear from the very beginning that his kingship could be only temporary. The time had come to give Israel its true king. History was on the move.

Why, in the first place, had God chosen a king from Binyomin?

We will first turn to Ramban at Bereishis 49:10. In this passage Ramban discusses the gift of the kingship that the Ribono shel Olam had given to Yehudah. In the course of his remarks he writes as follows:

וענין שאול היה, כי בעבור שדבר שאלת המלכות בעת ההיא נתעב אצל
הקדוש ברוך הוא, לא רצה להמליך עליהם מן השבט אשר לו המלכות שלא

יסור ממנו לעולמים, ונתן להם מלכות שעה ולזה רמז הכתוב שאמר אתן
לך מלך באפי ואקח בעברתי (הושע יג יא), שנתנו לו שלא ברצונו, ולכן
לקחו בעברתו, שנהרג הוא ובניו ונפסקה ממנו המלכות.

Why then was Shaul granted the original kingship? It
was because the Ribono shel Olam considered the request that a monarchy be established at that time, ill
conceived. Therefore, God did not want to grant them
a king from the tribe in whom the right to kingship was
formally vested. That would have resulted in a permanent investiture. But, under the circumstances, God
wished to grant only a temporary kingship. This is implied in Hosea 13:11, *I gave you a king in My anger, and took
the kingship away in My wrath.* This means that because
God's hand was, so to speak, forced, He did not permit
it to last. Shaul and his sons were killed and his royal line
was discontinued.

This Ramban gives us a general idea of why things developed
as they did, but we are still left short of any real understanding of the many parts that make up this story. Shaul came as
close to perfection as it is given to a human to be. The account
of his investiture as king makes clear that as a person, if not
from the point of view of his lineage, he was hugely qualified
for high office. *Now he had a son whose name was Shaul, who was
uniquely endowed and of pleasant appearance. From his shoulder upward he towered over all the people. There was no one in
Israel who was better than he* (I Shmuel 9:3). Why should such
a wonderful person have a position imposed upon him that he
had not sought and that, by definition, would have to end in
disappointment?[1]

In sum, we have two problems. Why, of all the tribes, was
the tribe of Binyomin chosen for this tragic, eventually truncated kingship? And why was Shaul the point man who had
to carry the burden?

I suspect that Binyomin was chosen because it was he from
among all the tribes who was most likely to be successful in
fighting Amalek, the task that would become immediately in-
cumbent upon the new king. He would be more empowered

than the others because he was the only one who had never bowed down to Eisav.[2] Moreover, Bava Basra 17a counts Binyomin as one of the four humans who were completely without sin and died only because death had been decreed upon Adam and his descendants. This combination of proud integrity and perfect piety would certainly recommend this tribe as the one from which a king, who for whatever reason could not be from Yehudah, should be chosen.

Shaul, too, just as his ancestor Binyomin had been, was without sin at the time of his investiture. This we know from Yoma 22b, which addresses I Shmuel 13:1: *Shaul was a year old when he became king.* The meaning is that at the ascension to the throne he was as innocent of sin as is a one-year-old child.[3] There appear to have been good and sufficient reasons that if a temporary king was to be chosen, that choice should fall upon the Binyominite Shaul.[4]

However, here we come to a paradox. Chazal feel that it was Shaul's very perfection that doomed him to failure.

אמר רב יהודה אמר שמואל מפני מה לא נמשכה מלכות בית שאול מפני
שלא היה בו שום דופי דאמר רבי יוחנן משום רבי שמעון בן יהוצדק אין
מעמידין פרנס על הציבור אלא אם כן קופה של שרצים תלויה לו מאחוריו
שאם תזוח דעתו עליו אומרין לו חזור לאחוריך.

R. Yehudah taught in Shmuel's name, "Why did Shaul's kingship not last? It was because there was no fault in him at all. For R. Yochanan taught in the name of R. Shimon ben Yehotzadak, 'We never appoint anybody as a leader over the community unless he is burdened by a "box of worms." We insist on this so that if his pride were ever to become overweening, we can tell him, "Look backward, be aware of your own serious imperfections."'"

(Yoma 22b)

Power can be addictive[5] and power without restraint can be catastrophic. It was better that a leader have reason to harbor some doubts about himself. Shaul, with his impeccable lineage leading to Binyomin, was not plagued by any doubts concerning his worth. By contrast, Dovid could never forget his descent from the Moabite Rus. He would never be in a position to take anything for granted.[6]

Now our assumptions in the previous paragraph are based upon Rashi's commentary to the Yoma passage we have just quoted. He takes *dofi,* which we translated as "fault," as referring to a less than stellar lineage. However, as Rashi himself interprets the word in numerous other places, it could be given a much broader meaning.[7] Shaul had no *dofi/faults* in the sense that he had no sins on his conscience. This is in striking contrast to Dovid whose past had not been free of shortcomings. Perhaps this is what the Gemara means when it says that Shaul was without *dofi.*

Of course in order to offer this explanation for the Yoma passage we would need to show why a personal acquaintance with the darker side of life appears to be desirable in a king. We shall take this up in the coming chapters.

At the beginning of this chapter we undertook to discuss the drama of Dovid's entry into Jewish history. We are now ready to do so. However, this deserves a chapter of its own. This is an exciting moment. Come, let us make the most of it.

FIVE

At the Cradle of the Dovidic Kingship

Now HaShem said to Shmuel, "How long will you continue to mourn for Shaul?...Fill your flask with oil and go! I will send you to Yishai who lives in Beis Lechem, for I have decided that one of his sons will be the king of My choice...Invite Yishai to take part in your feast; I will tell you what to do. Then you will anoint the one whom I shall point out to you."

(I Shmuel 16:1–3)

*T*here is a problem which concerns me, which none of the commentators who are currently available to me raises. Shmuel mourned Shaul's downfall deeply. That is not hard to understand. One would have to be possessed of a heart of stone not to be moved by the contemplation of so much promise ending in so blighted a life. Do not all of us share in Shmuel's grieving? So why does the Ribono shel Olam seem to condemn Shmuel's concern? And, if He does, why record His strictures? Do we really have to know the extent to which Shmuel erred?

It seems clear to me that the Ribono shel Olam's criticism has a bearing upon the story which is about to unfold. With a very different future beckoning, Shmuel was excessively focused upon the past. It was time for a changing of the guard. A Binyominite reign was about to fade into history; a scion from Yehudah would strike out on new paths, would pursue new goals, would be nurtured by new dreams. An inappropriate fixation upon Shaul would only prevent Shmuel from understanding Dovid. Shmuel's ideas should have been changing. History was not about to wait.[1]

God's fears were borne out. Initially Shmuel seemed bent upon finding another Shaul.

I suppose that Shmuel's attachment to the old standards explains why the Ribono shel Olam did not take him into His confidence. Why did Shmuel have to see all of Yishai's other sons only to discover that none of them was to be chosen? Why did the Ribono shel Olam not send him directly to Dovid? The answer must be that Shmuel had first to learn what was *not* good. Only then would he be able to appreciate correctly the nature and the destiny of the *malchus beis Dovid*.

Let us see whether we cannot throw some light upon the process by which the kingship passed from Binyomin to Yehudah.

ויהי בבואם וירא את אליאב ויאמר אך נגד יהוה משיחו. ויאמר יהוה אל שמואל אל תבט אל מראהו ואל גבה קומתו כי מאסתיהו כי לא אשר יראה האדם כי האדם יראה לעינים ויהוה יראה ללבב.

When they arrived he saw Eliav and said, "Surely His anointed one is standing before God!" But HaShem said to Shmuel, "Do not look at his appearance or at his regal stature, for I have rejected him. People are readily deceived by appearances. Man sees what his eyes behold but HaShem looks to the heart."

We follow Rashi.[2] Eliav's regal appearance leaves no doubt in Shmuel's mind that God's choice would fall upon this young man.

Before we can pick up the thread of the narrative we will have to make a short excursus. We must try to understand what made Shmuel err so badly. Did he really attach such importance to outward appearance? I suppose that we might defend his stance by recalling the language which the people had used when they asked for a king in the first place. *"Let us be like all the other nations. Let it be our king who judges us and who will lead us to war to fight our battles"* (I Shmuel 8:20). There was no very exalted thinking there. They simply wanted to be like everybody else. It makes sense to assume that they would only be satisfied with someone who fit their puerile dreams. We can understand Shmuel.

However, when we think about it carefully this explanation will really not do. We recall from I Shmuel 9:2 that when Shaul first appears upon the scene he is introduced to us by the anonymous narrator[3] as being good looking and taller than anybody else.[4] Quite literally there appears to be more to outward appearance than meets the eye.

Then there is the matter of God's *musar* to Shmuel in v. 7. *"Do not look at his appearance or at his regal stature, for I have rejected him. People are readily deceived by appearances. Man sees what his eyes behold but HaShem looks to the heart."* If we are correct, then Shmuel did not deserve this stricture. He had only wanted to accommodate what he perceived as the people's needs.

Shmuel must indeed have been impressed by Eliav's outer appearance. It appears to me that we can explain this only on the basis of R. Tzadok HaKohen of Lublin's assertion (Yisrael Kedoshim 6), that, in the world of the great figures who people TaNaCh, there was always an absolute congruence between essential nature and outer, physical form.[5] In that world, a handsome appearance conveyed a great deal. It pointed to harmonious balance and reflected an inner propensity towards the modesty, the purity of heart and the degree of God-fearing self abnegation which are prerequisites for Israel's kings.

We may safely assume that Shmuel thought that Eliav's outer perfection mirrored that of Shaul and that this implied that Eliav too had that same inner sense of what is right which marked Shaul as possessing the innocence of a year-old infant, as we learned in the previous chapter.

What then did God see in Eliav's heart that Shmuel had not detected with his normally penetrating vision? The answer may lie in the following passage from Menachos 109b. (See endnote 5 to the previous chapter.)

אמר ר' יהושע בן פרחיה בתחלה כל האומר עלה לה אני כופתו ונותנו לפני הארי עתה כל האומר לי לירד ממנה אני מטיל עליו קומקום של חמין שהרי שאול ברח ממנה וכשעלה בקש להרוג את דוד.

R. Yehoshua ben Perachiah taught: "Originally before I became a *nasi*, I would have thrown anybody to the lions who suggested that I should become a *nasi*. Now that I am a prince, I would pour a kettle of boiling water over anybody who would want to persuade me to give up my position. My proof is from Shaul, who originally fled from the prospect of becoming king, and in the end was willing to kill Dovid when Dovid threatened his kingship."

Maharal (Chidushei Aggada, there) contemplates the agony of one who has a kettle of scalding water poured over him. He believes that just so painful is the suffering of one who is brought face to face with his inadequacies, after he had been convinced that he was worthy of high office. Suddenly his world crashes about him and he is devastated. Even a Shaul, who had been victorious in every other struggle to the extent that as an adult he was still as innocent as a baby, succumbed before such an onslaught upon his self respect.

We can take this thought even further. His very guiltlessness made the sudden realization that he had failed even more unbearable. Great as Shaul's modesty must have been, and indeed it was very great as many incidents in his story make clear, it seems inevitable that when he was crowned king he felt a quiet sense of satisfaction at this vindication of a heroic life quietly and earnestly lived. He was human and we must assume that he had human feelings. How the lash of Shmuel's unsparing words must have cut: *"For HaShem has torn the kingship of Israel away from you and awarded it to your fellow who is better than you"* (I Shmuel 15:28).

This was a moment for which nothing in his blameless life could have prepared him. And indeed, at that crucial moment, he failed. This must have been what the Ribono shel Olam was telling Shmuel. "What do you see in Eliav which makes you so certain that he will be free of the great flaw which proved to be Shaul's undoing? I see into Eliav's heart and there is nothing there to make Me feel confident that he would not fail as abjectly as Shaul did."

We can word our conclusions as follows. The temporary kingship of Shevet Binyomin was well served by Shaul's piety. He was an ideal role model for his people. Had this been all that would have been required from the permanent kingship in Israel, Eliav, as evidenced by his tall stature and regal bearing, would have done as well. However, for the permanent kingship there are other requirements. We will find out more about these as we discover in the next chapter what Dovid possessed that Shaul did not. Come, we have much to do.

SIX

Florid—Though With Beautiful Eyes

Then Shmuel said to Yishai, "Can it be that there are no
more sons besides these?" He answered, "One youngster
is still missing; he is out in the pasture with the sheep."
So Shmuel said to Yishai, "Send for him that he may be
brought here; we will not begin the feast until he shall
have come." So he sent for him and he was brought. He
was of a florid complexion,[1] though with beautiful eyes
and a handsome appearance. So HaShem said, "Come,
anoint him for he is the one!"

(I Shmuel 16:11–12)

*A*lthough not stated explicitly, it seems obvious to
me that Yishai must have known, or at the very
least suspected, the purpose of Shmuel's visit. Still
he apparently had no intention to send for Dovid
until Shmuel demanded that he do so. He must have thought
that his youngest son could not be a serious candidate for the
kingship.

That appears to have been a serious misjudgment. How
could it be that a conscientious and wise father[2] would know
a precious son so imperfectly? How could he have been so
blind to the vast potential that was incubating within his own
family?[3]

What could have been the source of Yishai's error?

Perhaps Yishai knew his son well enough to recognize the
tumultuous battles that roiled within him. Perhaps he thought
that Shaul, who combined his own physical prowess with the
sweet innocence and serenity of a year-old infant, remained
the paradigm of the ideal king. Dovid, who as we will now
begin to trace, had to fight each spiritual battle fiercely, who
could never rest because he knew that to relax his guard for
even a moment would result in dreadful sin, could never—so
Yishai may have reasoned—be a trusted leader of the people.

But we have jumped ahead of ourselves. We have made
some very specific assumptions about Dovid's character with-

out offering any proof. You, dear reader, must be wondering what gives me the right to describe Dovid's character as I have done.

It is time to lay the foundations upon which the next few chapters are going to be based. It is time to begin to recognize Dovid not only as the slayer of wild beasts (I Shmuel 17: 34) and giants (I Shmuel 17: 49), not only as the victor of countless battles against Israel's enemies, but also, and more important, as the one who, after mighty struggles, gained mastery over himself. Each moral victory—and these were constant, punctuating his sublime life until the very end—came at a terrible cost.[4] For Dovid, the unblemished life did not come easily.

Let us begin to work out our subject in a more orderly fashion. Let us pick up where we left off earlier and see what happened when Dovid, answering his father's summons, appeared before Shmuel.

I have placed a paraphrase of the passage that describes this tension-filled moment at the beginning of this chapter, and if you are still with me, you must have trusted my rendering. Well, I hope that your trust has been well placed, but there is at least one phrase that I am going to have to justify to you. It is this: *He was florid,* THOUGH *with beautiful eyes and a handsome appearance.* That "though" is not as simple as it sounds. Here is why:

The Hebrew word that concerns us is *im*, in the phrase, *admoni* IM *yefei einayim.*[5] What does "*im*" convey? Is it "together with" or is it "in spite of"?[6] Rashi is silent. Radak opts for the earlier possibility. He notes that *im* is used as *and* at Nachum 3:12.

However, Malbim differs.

כי דוד היה אדמוני שגברה בו האדומה והוא בטבעו מוכן לשפיכת דם,
ומצד אחר נראה בו ג"כ רושמים טובים כי היה יפה עינים וטוב ראי – שזה
מורה על שהוא חד העיון וטוב המזג כמ"ש הטבעיים, ואם היה נשאר על
ההבחנה האנושית של שמואל היה מחליט היותו בלתי ראוי, אבל ה' יראה
ללבב וידע כי מטוב בחירתו יעשה אך משפט וצדקה, ובטבע האדמימות
הנטועה בו ישתמש ללחום מלחמות ה' ולהכרית מעיר ה' כל פועלי און,

וזה הנרצה בעיני ה' שהגם שנמצא נטיה רעה בטבעו הוא ימשול בה מצד
צדקתו וטוב בחירתו, וז"ש קום משחהו כי זה הוא – הנרצה לפני.

Dovid had a florid complexion, which indicates that he
would have a propensity toward murder. However, this
character trait not withstanding, his appearance also
boded well for good qualities for he had beautiful eyes
and a pleasant appearance....Now if Shmuel's human
observations would have been correct, Dovid, because
of these conflicting tendencies, would have had to be rejected [warring characteristics tend toward an undesir-
able instability]. But the Ribono shel Olam looks to the
heart and knew that Dovid, though torn, would master
both inclinations although, as they stand, they seem to be
in contradiction to each other. He would use the aggressive tendencies augured by his florid complexion only to
fight the wars of the Ribono shel Olam and to destroy all
evildoers. The pleasant aspects of his personality would
be applied to administering justice and charity. Now
that is precisely what the Ribono shel Olam wanted.
He wanted that despite those of his character traits that
tended toward the negative, he would, by using the disci-
pline of free choice, find the correct path to walk.

God, so Malbim maintains, wanted a warrior/king—not, at
least not in the first place, one who would fight Israel's enemies, but who would battle the destructive elements within
his own personality. The paradigm of the serene and pious
Shaul was good enough or perhaps even appropriate for the
temporary kingship that God granted *in His anger* (see chapter 4). For the long haul, or as we might put it, for the kingship
that would produce the Melech HaMoshiach, something
quite different was required. The very qualities that in Yishai's
eyes tended to disqualify his youngest son from consideration for the kingship—the fact that, in contrast to his settled
brothers, he seemed constantly embroiled in a maelstrom of
conflicting drives—were the very ones that the Ribono shel
Olam valued.

We have chosen to follow Malbim.[7]

We will devote chapter 8 to trying to discover why we could view a turbulent, really an unstable personality, as an advantage to the Melech HaMoshiach. Before we do that though, we will need to give some body to Malbim's theory. Is there any evidence to bear out that Dovid was indeed conflicted throughout his life? I have the feeling that we are at the threshold of some major discoveries.

Dovid and the Beis Hamikdash

*M*uch later, long after Dovid had become king, he judged that conditions were right[1] and that the time had come for him[2] to build the Beis HaMikdash. The story of how he approached Nathan the prophet with his idea and how Nathan conveyed to him God's message that not he but his son would be the one to build the temple, is told in II Shmuel, chapter 7, and in I Divrei HaYamim, chapter 17.[3] In neither account does the Ribono shel Olam explain why Dovid was not suited to this great task. However, in I Divrei HaYamim 22:8, Dovid reveals the reason to Shlomo: *But the word of HaShem came to me saying,"You have shed much blood and waged great wars; you shall not build a house for My name for you have shed much blood upon the ground before Me."*[4]

Now it is particularly interesting that Dovid prefaced his remarks to Shlomo with the statement that "HaShem came to me, saying...." Since there is no record of the Ribono shel Olam having spoken to Dovid on this matter, we must assume that this was a part of what Nathan had told him in God's name. However, we have what appears to be the full account of what Nathan said to Dovid in both the Shmuel and the Divrei HaYamim versions, and in neither of them are these considerations either stated or implied. It seems to me that we must conclude that Nathan never gave any reasons for God's denial of Dovid's dream, but that Dovid, on his own, worked out the implications. Dovid's self-knowledge was sufficiently acute that for him, Nathan's message as good as spelled out the explanation. Nothing else could justify the Ribono shel Olam's decision.

What precisely did Dovid know about himself that made the explanation obvious?

To answer this we must move to a *sugia* in Shabbos 30a, where a completely new dimension is introduced into the matter.

אמר דוד לפני הקדוש ברוך הוא רבונו של עולם מחול לי על אותו עון אמר
לו מחול לך אמר לו עשה עמי אות בחיי אמר לו בחייך איני מודיע בחיי
שלמה בנך אני מודיע כשבנה שלמה את בית המקדש ביקש להכניס ארון
לבית קדשי הקדשים דבקו שערים זה בזה אמר שלמה עשרים וארבעה
רננות ולא נענה פתח ואמר שאו שערים ראשיכם והנשאו פתחי עולם ויבא
מלך הכבוד רהטו בתריה למיבלעיה אמרו מי הוא זה מלך הכבוד אמר להו
ה' עזוז וגבור חזר ואמר שאו שערים ראשיכם ושאו פתחי עולם ויבא מלך
הכבוד מי הוא זה מלך הכבוד ה' צבאות הוא מלך הכבוד סלה ולא נענה
כיון שאמר ה' אלהים אל תשב פני משיחך זכרה לחסדי דוד עבדך מיד נענה
באותה שעה נהפכו פני כל שונאי דוד כשולי קדירה וידעו כל העם וכל
ישראל שמחל לו הקדוש ברוך הוא על אותו עון.

Dovid said to God, "Forgive me for having sinned [in the matter of Bas Sheva]."

God answered, "You are forgiven."

Dovid continued, "Send a sign while I am still alive that You have indeed forgiven me."

God answered, "There will be no sign during your lifetime. I will provide it once Shlomo becomes king."

[The sign came about in the following manner.] When Shlomo built the Beis HaMikdash he attempted to bring the ark into the Holy of Holies. The gates clung to one another and refused to open. Shlomo offered up many different prayers but was unable to move the gates. However when he said, "Oh HaShem, God, do not refuse your anointed one. Oh remember the pieties of Your servant Dovid" the gates immediately swung open.

Dovid's opponents were embarrassed; everybody saw that Dovid's sin had indeed been forgiven.

The story is a moving one, is it not? It turns out that although God had disqualified Dovid from building the Beis HaMikdash, in the end it was Dovid, not Shlomo, who really brought it into being. The implication is certainly that, at this point, the blood that Dovid had shed no longer stood in his way. If we combine this with the fact that this happened only after Dovid had died, we are left with the following proposition: Dovid's history of soldiering and killing disqualified him only while he was still alive; after he had died, they no longer stood in his way.

How are we to understand this? And by what legerdemain does the fact that Dovid was now able to put the finishing touch on the Beis HaMikdash become a sign that God had forgiven him for his less than admirable conduct in the matter of Bas Sheva? Dovid's disqualification as the builder of the Beis HaMikdash and his failings in the Bas Sheva incident had never before intersected in any way. What brings them together now?

We have come to a point at which we must get to know Dovid HaMelech a little better. We will learn to understand something of the nature of the many wars he was called upon to execute, and the killings that necessarily were a part of these martial exploits. At the same time we must examine the strange concept that an event that happened during Shlomo's reign was able, retroactively, to act as a sign that Dovid had been forgiven for sins that had been committed many years earlier.

First, then, let us turn to the wars.

Here are a few lines from an extensive treatment in R. Tzadok HaKohen's Tzidkas HaTzadik, section 244:

פי' כל מלחמותיו הי' בניצוח היצר כפי מה שנצח ליצר כך נצח לאומות שהכל אחד.

It must be understood that all the wars that Dovid executed were reflections of the inner struggles that were taking place within himself. To the extent that he was able to be victorious over his own baser drives, to that extent he won victories over his enemies.

The military engagements, entailing as they did much killing and suffering, were no more than the outer form of the constant inner struggles that were Dovid's lot in life. Dovid did indeed lead a blameless life, but his victories over his base inclinations were just that; they were victories only to the extent that with superhuman strength and effort he cowed them into impotence. Until the very end of his life he did not succeed in eliminating them completely. Because of this, there was always the chance that some day they might overwhelm him. This inherent instability disqualified him from building the Beis HaMikdash, which, by its nature, required a permanent and unshakable peace.[5]

So the building of the Beis HaMikdash was left to Shlomo HaMelech. In the charge that Dovid made to the leaders of the people shortly before his death (I Divrei HaYamim 22:18–19), Dovid told them:

הלא יהוה אלהיכם עמכם והניח לכם מסביב כי נתן בידי את ישבי הארץ ונכבשה הארץ לפני יהוה ולפני עמו. עתה תנו לבבכם ונפשכם לדרוש ליהוה אלהיכם וקומו ובנו את מקדש יהוה האלהים להביא את ארון ברית יהוה וכלי קדש האלהים לבית הנבנה לשם יהוה.

"Surely HaShem your God is with you and He will leave you at peace with all the enemies who surround you, for He has given the inhabitants of the land into my hand and the land has been subdued before HaShem and before His people. Now set your hearts and souls to seeking HaShem your God. Rise and build a sanctuary of HaShem God so that the ark...may be brought into the house that is to be built for the name of HaShem."

In light of what we have learned from R. Tzadok, the meaning is clear. To the extent that the country was at peace with its neighbors, to that extent Dovid had been victorious in his inner struggles. He had finally attained the spiritual stability that, had it appeared earlier in his life, would have enabled him to fulfill his dream of building the Beis HaMikdash. However, for him it had come too late. It would be Shlomo who reaped what Dovid, by his prodigious efforts, had sown.

This understood, it becomes clear that we must view the reigns of Dovid and Shlomo as a continuum, the parts of which relate to each other as do labor and rest, effort and fruition. Dovid had finally wrested peace and harmony from the rigors of battle. Shlomo's reign was to be the expression of that triumph.[6]

We have laid the groundwork for finding solutions to the

conundrums that troubled us earlier in this essay. We wondered why the sign that Dovid had been forgiven should have been given only after he had already died. The insights that we have garnered from R. Tzadok provide the obvious answer. The total cleansing from any disposition to negative inclinations came about only with Dovid's death. Before then he had not yet attained the required equilibrium. That it was Shlomo who built the Temple gates, but the merit of Dovid that opened them, tells the whole story.

Our other problem was the sudden appearance of the Bas Sheva episode in a matter to which it had no obvious connection. Dovid had been denied permission to build the Beis HaMikdash because of the blood he had shed. Nowhere in TaNaCh is there any indication that the Bas Sheva indiscretions had any connection.

However, once we realize that the wars that plagued Dovid's reign were nothing more than the tangible expression of the inner turmoil of his soul, the solution is self-evident. Dovid's inner conflicts revolved around the very drives and inclinations that led him astray in these tragic occurrences (see Sefer Tehilim, chapter 51).[7] It was they that allowed him no rest and drove him to ever greater heights of heroism both in his personal battles and in the wars waged against Israel's enemies. When peace was finally attained in Shlomo's reign—a peace born of Dovid's mighty victories—this showed that these drives had also finally been laid to rest. The incident with Bas Sheva had finally been relegated to history. With no deleterious effects remaining, the sin had been forgiven.

Malbim's perception of Dovid as a man who, during his lifetime, was conflicted by roiling passions seems amply confirmed. We can now move forward with our plan to find out in what way this turmoil in Dovid's soul could have been viewed as an advantage to one who carried within himself the future Melech HaMoshiach.

Shepherds as Judges

*Y*ou might want to glance back at chapter 3 to re-
fresh your memory concerning Yechezkel, chapter 34. This is the passage in which Israel's failed
kings appear as lazy self-serving shepherds who
care nothing for their charges but everything for themselves. I
now want to revisit that chapter and examine the Ribono shel
Olam's promise that in the future He will no longer delegate
the care of His flock to others. He, by Himself, will assume the
role of shepherd.

Let us look at the following passage.

אני ארעה צאני ואני ארביצם נאם אדני יהוה. את האבדת אבקש ואת
הנדחת אשיב ולנשברת אחבש ואת החולה אחזק ואת השמנה ואת
החזקה אשמיד ארעה במשפט. ואתנה צאני כה אמר אדני יהוה הנני שפט
בין שה לשה לאילים ולעתודים....לכן כה אמר אדני יהוה אליהם הנני אני
ושפטתי בין שה בריה ובין שה רזה....והושעתי לצאני ולא תהיינה עוד לבז
ושפטתי בין שה לשה.

I will look after My sheep and I will lay them to rest.
It will be I Who will search for the lamb that has been
lost; I Who will restore the one that was made to stray.
I will bind up their broken limbs and attend to the sick
among them. The fat and strong ones [who tend to push
the others around] I will drive away. I will apportion my
care *justly*.[1]

Thus says my Lord, "You are My flock. I am ready
to *judge* between sheep and sheep, among the rams
and among the he-goats....Behold I am ready to *judge*
between the healthy sheep and the wasted ones....I will
save My sheep and they will no longer fall prey to others,
I will *judge* between one sheep and the next."

(Yechezkel 34:15–22)

Strange, is it not? Why the constant reiteration of the shepherd as judge? Without these repeated references, the pastoral

scene that Yechezkel depicts would be idyllic. The shepherd is the concerned protector of his flock. He is kind; he is alert; he cares. It is not as detailed a picture as the one painted by the well-known Tehilim, chapter 23, *HaShem is my shepherd, I shall not want*, but, if we could dismiss the repeated references to the shepherd as judge, it would be fully in consonance with it. The Tehilim passage mentions nothing of any altercation between the sheep that would require a judge to sort things out. Nothing disturbs the serenity that the psalm so successfully portrays. Why, in the Yechezkel passage, should it be necessary to describe the shepherd as judge no less than three times within seven verses?

Moreover, in the earlier part of the Yechezkel chapter where the prophet describes the deficiencies of the lazy shepherds, he does not mention that they were unconcerned with executing justice among the sheep. Why then would the Shepherd of the future need to insist so firmly that He will not be derelict in the exercise of this responsibility?

The matter becomes clear when we consider that the Yechezkel passage is interested in the shepherds only to the extent that they can be used as a metaphor for Israel's kings. So the ability to administer justice responsibly looms large. Kings do need to function as judges. Rambam makes this point in Hilchos Melachim 4:10:

שאין ממליכין מלך תחלה אלא לעשות משפט ומלחמות שנאמר ושפטנו מלכנו ויצא לפנינו ונלחם את מלחמותינו.

For there is no purpose in crowning a king other than that he should administer justice and fight wars. We know this from the request that the people made of Shmuel, "That our king might judge us and lead us into the wars that we will have to fight."

Nevertheless, a simple reading of TaNaCh can show that for some kings this function was more central than for others. Thus, for example, there is no biblical record of Dovid having functioned as judge while for Shlomo this activity seems to have been of inordinate importance. We may legitimately wonder what role *mishpat* is expected to play in the rule of the Melech HaMoshiach.

Let us consider Yeshayahu's vision in chapter 11.

ויצא חטר מגזע ישי ונצר משרשיו יפרה. ונחה עליו רוח יהוה רוח חכמה ובינה רוח עצה וגבורה רוח דעת ויראת יהוה. והריחו ביראת יהוה ולא למראה עיניו ישפוט ולא למשמע אזניו יוכיח.

A shoot shall grow out from the stump of Yishai, a twig shall sprout forth from his roots. HaShem's spirit will rest upon him, a spirit of wisdom and understanding, a spirit of counsel and valor, a spirit of knowledge and fear of HaShem. Moreover, God will imbue him[2] with fear of HaShem, that he will not [need to] judge by the evidence of his eyes, nor decide by the evidence that he will hear.

(Yeshayahu 11:1–5)

It would be wonderful if we could spend the time to analyze each of these magnificent phrases in detail. Shabbos 31a teaches us that one day we will be called upon to give an accounting of the extent to which we longed for the coming of Moshiach.[3] I have the feeling that this passage, so rich in promise and anticipation, could help us along in an area in which some of us are less than perfect. However, now is not the time for such musings. In this essay we must remain firmly focused on the task we have set ourselves. We have set out to discover what role the administration of justice is to play in the reign of the Melech HaMoshiach.

The Yeshayahu passage seems to anticipate a significant one. Let us try to understand what the prophet meant when he said, *Moreover, God will imbue[4] him with fear of HaShem, thus that he will not judge by the evidence of his eyes, nor decide by the evidence that he will hear.*

As it stands it does not seem to convey much to us. Let us commit ourselves to some heavy thinking.

The big test is going to be whether we can produce an accurate translation of *veharicho*.[5] We know that we are dealing with the *hiph'il,* the causative voice. That is useful but not sufficient. We still need to work out whether this verb derives from *rei'ach*, "smell," or *ru'ach*, "spirit." Now, when we consider that in the *pasuk* immediately preceding this one, the word *ru'ach* occurs three times, we would certainly be inclined to assume that *harich* means "to imbue with spirit." That is, in fact, how Rashi takes it.

However, the fact is that while we do find verbs formed from *rei'ach*,[6] we never (except perhaps here) find *ru'ach* as a verb. I assume that it is because of this that Radak disagrees with Rashi and opts for *rei'ach* rather than *ru'ach* as the root. If so, the translation would be *to imbue with a sense of smell.*

Now what could this possibly mean? Why would the Melech HaMoshiach need to be endowed with a particularly acute sense of smell?

Radak solves this problem by reading the phrase as a metaphor. It stands in for a lightning-like, intuitive grasp of what is right and what is not. Of all the senses, that of smell is "lightest."[7] I take a whiff and my brain immediately identifies what it is that I am smelling. Because of this, the sense of smell more than any other can serve as a metaphor for an effortless perception of reality. The phrase conveys the idea that the Melech HaMoshiach would be endowed with a fail-safe instinct that would tell him immediately, without requiring either observation or reliance upon testimony, who among two litigants is right and who is wrong.

Chazal appear to agree with Radak. Sanhedrin 93b tells the story of Bar Kochba, the would-be Messiah. When he declared himself, the rabbis decided to put his claim to the test. Based on our verse they had concluded that the true Moshiach would *morach veda'in*,[8] "sniff" and "judge." Bar Kochba's claim would stand or fall by whether he could persuade them that he had this ability. They found that he was unable to make such snap decisions and withdrew their support for him.

We are now ready to wonder why the Melech HaMoshiach should have to be endowed with this intuitive faculty. It certainly seems unlikely that there is an anticipation of much personal litigation in Messianic times. Rambam (Melachim 12:5) tells us that *there will be neither jealousy nor competition because anything desirable will be in plentiful supply and all luxuries will be as readily available as the dust of the earth. People will be interested only in gaining a closer understanding of the Ribono shel Olam.* So it seems that forensic skills ought not to be high on the list of qualities demanded of the Melech HaMoshiach.

It seems to me that this ability is related to Chazal's teaching (Chagigah 12a) that the light which the Ribono shel Olam created on the first day would have enabled men to see from one end of the world to the other.[9] The Gemara teaches that the Ribono shel Olam withdrew this light from general use because He saw that the faculty to apprehend all of existence without let or hindrance could easily be abused by wicked people. Therefore, this wondrous light would be hidden, kept safe through the ages, and be made available once more to the tzadikim who will arise among us in the future. I surmise, though I cannot claim to have any source for my assumption, that the Yeshayahu passage hints at this primordial light when it anticipates that the Melech HaMoshiach will be imbued with the ability to judge intuitively.[10]

If all this is true, then *morach veda'in* in the sense of an intuitive feel for who among litigants is right and who wrong, is only the tip of a vast iceberg. Rather it describes wisdom so profound and so far-reaching that it comprehends all that is given to the human mind to grasp "from one end of the world to the other." Nothing will be hidden from the Melech HaMoshiach, because he will truly be a "Melech," a ruler over the entire range of human experience. His will be a new take on the blessing that God bestowed upon Adam (Bereishis 1:28), *fill the land and* CONQUER *it.* His will be a conquest of the spirit, a conquest of understanding, a conquest of perception and differentiation.

We have reached a point at which we can return to the issues that we raised in chapter 6. We learned from Malbim that Dovid's turbulent personality, the conflicting drives that left him no rest, far from disqualifying him from the kingship, were the very elements that God treasured in him. We wondered why such an unsettled personality should be seen as an advantage for the kingship. It now seems to me that for the kind of intuitive discrimination between good and evil with which the Melech HaMoshiach is to be endowed, a sophisticated knowledge of the contours and range, of the depth and inspired cunning of evil, is an absolute requirement. The innocence of a small child is indeed a thing of beauty. Shaul must have been loved and admired by the people. It was under the influence of this model that Yishai felt that there would be little purpose in introducing Dovid to Shmuel. Indeed Shmuel, by his immediate assumption that Eliav was to be the chosen one, showed that he had not yet grasped that the new monarchy was to be radically different from that which had been vested in Shaul.

But the Ribono shel Olam had determined that it was time for the much-conflicted Dovid to make his entry into history. Israel's permanent monarchy was to be built and developed on the basis of a thorough knowledge and understanding of man's fragility and vulnerability and of the chasm that divides good from evil. For that a "Dovid" was needed.

We will now begin a new phase of our contemplation of Dovid's life. We will try to examine some of the episodes that caused him much heartache and that contributed, to a greater or lesser extent, to his becoming that figure in our history who taught us the efficacy of teshuvah as it had never been taught before (Mo'ed Katan 16b).[11]

NINE

The Dovid of Shmuel and the Dovid of Tehilim

We are about to embark upon some very, very serious NaCh learning. We have the time, so let us do it right. Let us, for now, stay away from the actual material we are going to study and, instead, lay down some of the ground rules that will govern our research.

Our interest will be directed mainly at Sefer Shmuel, the historical account[1] of Dovid's life. Much of our analysis will center upon the differences between it and Sefer Divrei HaYamim in describing those events upon which we intend to focus. As we engage in this form of learning, it is important that we bear in mind that the Ribono shel Olam's Torah is not a history book. When we read secular history and happen upon two sources that contradict each other, we simply assume that the two accounts are the work of different authors and we do not spend time or energy attempting to reconcile them. In TaNaCh such an approach is disallowed. *Eilu ve'eilu divrei Elokim Chaim*, these and those are the words of the living God, and room must be made so that both can be legitimately accommodated.

Once all this is understood, it is time to spend a few moments providing a *hashkafah* background to the analysis that we are about to undertake.

We will be dealing with events that punctuated Dovid's turbulent life and particularly those that, in aggregate, may be said to have had an impact upon the tragic story of Dovid's meeting with Bas Sheva. Again and again we will be struck by the many wrong choices Dovid seems to have made and we will begin to wonder why, in view of these many apparent failings, it was just him whom the Ribono shel Olam chose to represent the ideal of Jewish kingship. We must not, however, lose sight of the fact that we possess a powerful commentary on Dovid's life, one that will allow us access to a Dovid of whose existence Sefer Shmuel tells us practically nothing. If we think of Sefer Shmuel without Sefer Tehilim, we are looking at only half the story. It is in Sefer Tehilim that we can meet the true Dovid.

At this point, I am going to quote from Dr. Henry Biberfeld's *David, King of Israel* (Cleveland, Jerusalem, New York: The Spero Foundation, 1963).[2]

> King David's biography as told in the historical books gives only the surface outline of his life. It is a one-dimensional story describing his journey along the stormy road of persecution and jealousy through the valleys of betrayal and treachery, to the soaring heights of regal achievement and love. But the story does not tell what went on below the surface; of the tempests and upheavals, of the visions of supreme bliss and harmony[3] in David's soul. Only rarely do indications of the existence of these hidden worlds flash into the action flow of the narrative. Like geysers bursting forth in sudden and explosive fury, indicating the tremendous forces constrained in subterranean secrecy, those brief episodes reveal the magnitude and power of the forces at work behind the events of David's life.
>
> David's real life is recorded in the psalms. This is the true mirror of his being, reflecting every phase of his life. If the historical books show the outward contours of his image, the psalms probe the deepest secrets. The psalms are his world, the world of the idea of God with all its variety. It is a world detached from and beyond the material sphere. Hence allusions to actual events occur only rarely in psalms. The historical books provide the form to be filled in with idea and experience.
>
> We cannot expect such a "biography of an idea" to conform to the usual pattern of history. The life of the idea progresses in a reality above space and time. Experience, memory, hope—all the tools of the mind—lift ideas out of their setting and transpose them into a reality where the laws of spatial order and temporal succession are deprived of their absoluteness. In the transactions of the

mind, time and space are but two of a limitless number of concepts and rather less real than many others.
Experience, the inner absorption of an event, makes it
independent of the flux of time. It rescues the event from
the stream of outer reality and anchors it to imperish-
able moorings. The event becomes part of eternity. The
present, itself a fictitious point of arrest in time, blooms
into eternity through the intensifying power of a joyous
or grievous experience.

Nor is experience restrained as to spatial relations. The
eye of the mind may bridge vast distances. Memory may
store away a location once visited and conjure it up at
will. Like slides in a projector, places, persons, and events
appear and vanish at the bidding of our imagination.

Man's capacity for experience is an independent and
selective force. Its power does not directly derive from the
potential of the event experience. A whispered word, a
fleeting thought, a facial expression may strike our mental chords with the impact of a hammer blow. The seed
of an experience may drift into our minds unnoticed,
sinking its roots in the subconscious only to reawaken
later and fill our active cognizance to the exclusion of all
other perceptions. On the other hand, events that take
place under most impressive outward circumstances
may bypass the gateway to the world of experience and
disappear forever into the pit of oblivion.

True experience is a fusion of certain elements of an
event and responding functions of the mind; the accord of the two causes the experience. Event and mind
are like two instruments playing a musical theme at the
same time. Each at times may lead as others merely accompany. Thus sometimes the event is the predominant
partner, while the mind merely offers a passive response.
Or the event may be inconspicuous and obscure, yet the
lens of a searching mind magnifies it into vast proportions. Events of universal and immediate significance
arouse the participation even of the crudest and most
sluggish of minds, while the alert and reacting imagina-

tion finds significance even in the bypaths of life. Birth and death, war and peace, material success or failure become experiences in everyone's life; but only the chosen few develop deep experiences from the harmony and rhythm of the workings of nature. David's mind, responsive as no other, found in the omnipresence of God the one experience that became the dominant force in his life, the atmosphere and living-space of his existence.

When the supreme "event" of the idea of God was perceived by David, an experience was born of such singular force that it reverberates through the ages. The psalms are the record of that great union, when the impact of the omnipresence of God struck the responsive chords of David's being. From the moment when "the spirit of God came upon David" it never again left him entirely.[4] It spread and grew in him until his whole person, soul and body, was suffused with it. David's reactions to the erratics of life were no longer his own. The divine in David thought, felt, spoke, and acted through him. The inner history of the life of David, his true biography, was called Tehilim, "reflection," for it is all reflections of the divine in the clear mirror of his soul.

In the psalms we find all that we look for in vain in the books describing David's outward life. Triumphs and tragedies, periods of calm and of unrest, of supreme confidence and hopeless despair, mystic surrender and moral reflections, universal love and implacable wrath, find expression in the psalms. They have words like thunderbolts or the whisper of a breeze, raging fire or soothing rain, fragrant flowers or corrosive acid, spanning the whole range of human experience.

Tradition tells how a harp that hung above David's bed began to play when the soft breeze of the predawn stirred its strings. Thus nature, the profusion of phenomena filling the world, made the chords of David's soul sing. One unending melody reverberates from it— God. This universal theme resounds from all directions of the cosmos. Space is filled with it, for "The heavens declare the glory of God" and "the earth is the Lord's." Time proclaims it, for: "Day unto day uttereth speech and night unto night showeth knowledge." Nature is but one aspect of the divine, null and void without the life giving presence of His might.

You, dear reader, will agree that this is an extremely powerful piece. As I read it just now, it occurred to me to wonder why Sefer Shmuel seems to ignore completely, or almost completely, those aspects of Dovid's history that come to life in Sefer Tehilim. None, or almost none, of Dovid's sublime compositions intrude upon the narrative in Sefer Shmuel. By resolutely refusing entry to "Dovid, the sweet singer of Israel's songs" into the stories of "Dovid the king, the warrior, and the would-be builder of God's Beis HaMikdash," Shmuel[5] seems to be withholding a significant part of Dovid's life. An incomplete picture is a false picture. Many *mizmorim* in Sefer Tehilim begin with an introductory verse that indicates the occasion upon which this particular psalm was composed or sung or said. The most prosaic events in Dovid's life were often set to music.[6] This singer/warrior lived a totally integrated life. Why do we look in vain in Sefer Shmuel for the "whole" Dovid?

The answer, to the extent that I am able to suggest one, deserves a chapter of its own. Come, let us forge on together.

TEN

A Closer Look at Sefer Shmuel

*T*he questions which we raised in the previous chapter force us to come to grips with some very fundamental issues concerning Sefer Shmuel. Our task is nothing less than attempting to understand what Shmuel wanted to accomplish by leaving us this literary record of the beginnings of the monarchy. Among *ehrliche yidden* it is surely axiomatic that a book which was canonized as part of TaNaCh cannot simply be regarded as a history of the period. It is Torah and demands that it be learned—not simply read—with all the serious commitment which we would lavish on a *parsha* in Chumash. [1]

The fact itself that much of the Davidic saga appears twice in TaNaCh, in Shmuel (Nevi'im) and in Divrei HaYamim (Kesuvim), and that there are many differences between the two accounts indicates that the two books had different agendas. [2] In this essay I would like to take a closer look at Sefer Shmuel.

I suspect that Shmuel gave a great deal of thought to the problem of persuading us to read this book in the spirit in which he wanted us to understand it. Certainly there was enough drama in Dovid's tumultuous life to make for gripping reading without the reader ever having to grapple with dimensions of meaning and implications which were not literally expressed in the language. But Shmuel wanted more, much more than that from his readers. [3]

I believe that what we will call the "Ending Section" of Sefer Shmuel provided Shmuel with the tool which he needed. It consists of four segments, three of which contribute to a correct understanding of all the narrative chapters which precede them.

Chapter 21 closes the historical section of the book. It is followed by four segments which we will number 1–4. We will then discuss each of these segments and try to understand if and how it contributes to a more profound understanding of the entire book.

Here is how the ending of the book is structured.

1. The first segment, contained in chapter 22, is a psalm which, with certain variations, parallels psalm 18 in Sefer Tehilim. Dovid is said to have recited this psalm *on the day that HaShem delivered him from the hand of all his enemies and from the hand of Shaul*. We will need to enquire why Shmuel felt that this particular composition was an appropriate opening for the Ending Section of Sefer Shmuel.

2. The second segment comprises the first seven verses of chapter 23. It consists of another poetic composition[4] which, in contrast to the earlier segment, did not find its way into the Book of Psalms. The language is unusually opaque and we will have to work hard to discover its message. Of course we will also have to determine its function in this closing section of the book.

3. The rest of the chapter is then taken up by the third segment, a listing of Dovid's *giborim*, the heroes who were a part of Dovid's retinue. In our discussion, we will learn that all these military virtuosos were also great Torah scholars. That, of course, has implications which we will attempt to uncover as we go along.

A similar list appears in II Divrei HaYamim chapter 11 verses 10–47. Chapter 11 is part of the narrative section of the book; it is in no way an ending. This fact will make our analysis difficult. We will be trying to understand the difference in the approach to this significant list displayed by the two books. Why did Shmuel reserve it as a part of the Ending Section when he could just as well have made it a part of Dovid's story?

4. Chapter 24 is the final segment of the Ending Section; it brings the book to its close. It is the story of an ill-fated census which Dovid undertook, and which was to bring great suffering upon the Jewish people.

It really does not seem to belong here. Both in style and content it is a straightforward accounting of a major event in Dovid's reign, one that ought to have been recorded earlier as a part of the Dovidic saga. Why was just this event segregated from all the others which punctuated Dovid's stormy life? Why use it to bring the book to its close when each of the other three segments in the Ending Section would have seemed to us to be a more logical ending for the book?

Our analysis will conclude that segments 1, 2, and 3 can be viewed as a commentary upon the earlier, narrative sections, and are therefore positioned advantageously. We will have to find a different solution for the fourth segment.

Herewith our thoughts on each of these four segments. We will first examine the ones which we have numbered 1, 3, and 4, leaving number 2, which for our purposes seems to me to be the most significant, to the end.

1. We will begin our analysis with the psalm which is the first segment in the Ending Section. There is something puzzling about the fact that this should be the only one of the one hundred and fifty psalms that comprise Sefer Tehilim which has found a place in Shmuel. As we noted in the previous chapter, many psalms in Sefer Tehilim are associated with events which are described in Shmuel. For reasons which we do not yet understand,[5] none of these appear in Shmuel where these events are described. Why is this psalm different from all the others?

The psalm is introduced with an opening verse: *Dovid addressed the words of this song to HaShem, on the day that HaShem had saved him from the hand of all his enemies and from the hand of Shaul.*[6]

For our purposes we will assume Abarbanel's explanation of these words. This was a song which Dovid sang on many different occasions ("from the hand of *all* his enemies.") Whenever he was helped or saved by the Ribono shel Olam, this would be the song through which he chose to express his gratitude. It is for this reason that Sefer Shmuel does not attach it to any particular point in Dovid's life. It was a composition upon which he drew constantly.[7]

If none of the other psalms fit naturally into Sefer Shmuel, this one needed to be there. It is an indispensable commentary upon the narrative sections. It serves as a link between the Dovid of Shmuel and the Dovid of Tehilim. The utterly human, very fallible king of the narratives, the apparently failed parent who found so little *nachas* from so many of his children, is revealed through Tehilim to have been the one who rendered all the songs which were ever, or will ever be, lodged in Israel's heart, with the delight[8] that has kept Tehilim alive for us throughout the fearful nights of our *galus*.[9] Each difficult moment of his life was an opportunity to meet the Ribono shel Olam on yet another plane, to turn the occasional dross of everyday life into the pure gold of experiencing the closeness to God which defined his true, inner life.

Let us for a moment imagine that we would have had only Sefer Shmuel in our TaNaCh and not Sefer Tehilim. Would we not have had a completely distorted picture of Dovid? There[10] were so many errors, so much that was done that had better been left undone. We would never have realized that here was a man who had no existence outside the meeting of God in prayer,[11] a mighty warrior who, nevertheless, knew no other value than peace.[12] [13]

By the simple expedient of including this psalm in his book, Shmuel HaNavi teaches us what, in essence, the story which he tells us is all about. It is about the truth that even very great men can sin—without impugning their greatness or cutting them off from their source of inspiration. Perhaps more importantly, that even sinning man can be great—if he is able to summon the energy which true Teshuvah demands.[14]

3. The list of Dovid's *giborim*, the warriors by whom he was surrounded, and the exploits which were associated with each one of them, requires careful analysis. The underlying theme, as it is understood and described in many different *midrashim*, centers upon the fact that with each one of them, their heroism and valor on the field of battle was paralleled by an equally outstanding performance while they were learning Torah in the Beis HaMidrash. In the confines of this small book there is no room for such detailed examination. The interested reader can consult my Divrei HaYamim commentary in the Artscroll TaNaCh series, volume 1, chapter 11 where, to the best of my ability, I have examined the sources.

I believe that Shmuel reserved the listing of these *giborim* until the Ending Section for much the same reason that he included the psalm which we discussed above. It leads us, albeit by a different route, to the same realization. Dovid's entire life was lived at two different levels; he was the lead actor in two dramas which played themselves out on two stages. The wars which are portrayed in Sefer Shmuel's pages were real. The blood that was shed, the pain of defeat and the elation of victory, all were experienced as described in TaNaCh. But for all that, they were no more than a surface reality. At a deeper and truer level the ebb and flow of battle was a metaphor for the exigencies of the struggle for creative understanding in the Beis HaMidrash, the *milchamto shel Torah*,[15] the struggle for knowledge. The sword which Dovid's *giborim* wielded so effectively against their enemies was essentially no more than the outer form of the sharpness of an intellect which was harnessed to storm ramparts of ignorance and insensitivity.

The list of the *giborim* seems to point to the same hidden strata of experiences to which the psalm which we discussed earlier gives body. We understand why it was given a place of honor in the Ending Section.

4. The fourth segment of the Ending Section, the story of Dovid's ill-fated census which brings the book to its close, is a different matter entirely. It can certainly not be viewed as a kind of commentary on the book as can the first two segments. If we were to attempt some mental gymnastics to try and pummel it into that grouping, we would, I think, end up on the wrong side of the truth. We must try to find a different approach to explain this unexpected placement.

It seems to me that the following suggestion may have some merit. We have already learned above that Sefer Divrei HaYamim covers the same historical period, the story of the monarchy from Dovid through the destruction of the first Temple, as do Sefer Shmuel together with Sefer Melachim. We also noted that there are many minor and not so minor differences between the two books on many details. A discussion of these differences is, I believe, important. However, I cannot undertake it in the framework of this small book, but suggest that the interested reader might want to check out my Divrei HaYamim commentary which is a part of the Artscroll TaNaCh series. Here we will note only that one of the very major differences between the two books is their treatment of the census story.

Chapter 24 of II Shmuel, the chapter which closes the book, contains the story of the census up to the point at which Dovid brings a sacrifice to God, thereby causing the plague, which had earlier been raging as a result of the unauthorized census, to stop. The book makes no mention of the fact that Dovid determined that the place where he brought this sacrifice would be the location at which Shlomo's Beis HaMikdash was to be built.

By contrast, Divrei HaYamim makes much of that aspect of the story. It is clearly the climax towards which the entire episode was moving. Divrei HaYamim then goes on to add no less than fifteen more chapters which detail the various preparations which Dovid then made in anticipation of the Beis HaMikdash which Shlomo would build. None of this is even hinted at in Shmuel.

We may conjecture why Shmuel should have ignored this highly significant aspect of Dovid's life. As noted above, this little book is not the place for such an analysis. However, this strange omission does hand us a key which can help us explain the strange positioning of this story. Perhaps Shmuel put it at the very end of the book to hint that it should be viewed as the beginning of the Shlomo era rather than as the last significant event in Dovid's reign. It is as though Shmuel is telling us, "This is as far as I can take you. However, you are standing at a beginning rather than at an end. Some day, someone other than I will provide the history of Shlomo's kingship. Know then, dear reader, that that story really begins here."

We are now finally ready to approach the second, and in my opinion the most difficult, segment of the Ending Section. Our analysis deserves a chapter of its own. Come, let us journey on together.

Dovid's "Final Words"

*T*his chapter will be devoted to an analysis of the second segment of the Ending Section of Sefer Shmuel. We have discussed the other three segments in the previous chapter.

Before we do anything else, we should look at the text.

א. ואלה דברי דוד האחרנים נאם דוד בן ישי ונאם הגבר הקם על משיח אלהי יעקב ונעים זמרות ישראל.

ב. רוח יהוה דבר בי ומלתו על לשוני.

ג. אמר אלהי ישראל לי דבר צור ישראל מושל באדם צדיק מושל יראת אלהים.

ד. וכאור בקר יזרח שמש בקר לא עבות מנגה ממטר דשא מארץ.

ה. כי לא כן ביתי עם אל כי ברית עולם שם לי ערוכה בכל ושמרה כי כל ישעי וכל חפץ כי לא יצמיח.

ו. ובליעל כקוץ מנד כלהם כי לא ביד יקחו.

ז. ואיש יגע בהם ימלא ברזל ועץ חנית ובאש שרוף ישרפו בשבת.

As usual, we will offer a translation. However, you will find that this translation is very different from the ones that you have read in the rest of this book. You will notice that in the English rendering many of the words are italicized. These are words that have no parallel in the text but needed to be included to make sense of what is being said. The phrases which we have inserted, have been chosen from various commentators with an eye to making the passage as understandable as possible, but without any particular system. The main consideration was to fill the gaps. The unusually choppy way in which this psalm is written will be the subject of the analysis which we will offer below.

These are the final words of Dovid:
[These are] the words of Dovid son of Yishai, the words of him who has been raised on high. [He is the one] anointed by Yaakov's God, the one who lends delight to Israel's songs.

The spirit of HaShem has spoken in me; His words are on my tongue.

The God of Israel spoke, the Rock of Israel spoke to me, *He said that I should become* a ruler over "Man" *and further that I should be a* righteous ruler *imbued with* the fear of God.

My power would spread as does the morning light when the sun begins to shine, a light that is never darkened. *It will be brighter than the light which is reflected when* rain drops upon the grasses.

For certainly my house *will not be like a darkened light* with God, for He has made an eternal covenant with me, *being aware of all my needs* well ordered and protected. *No one will ever* sprout forth *to usurp my kingship.*

But the wicked shall all be raked aside like thorns. For no one will take them in his hand.

Whoever would touch them would have to clothe himself in armor and provide himself with a spear. Wherever they make their home they must be burned.

As explained above, the words and phrases which are italicized are those which must be added to make sense of the text. However, it must be admitted that they are no more than a kind of first aid. The fact is that they are, so to speak, snatched out of the air. They do not appear in the Hebrew. In order to help you, dear reader to see just how incomplete the text actually appears, I will provide it once more but this time without the fillers which I suggested.

These are the final words of Dovid:

The words of Dovid son of Yishai, the words of he who has been raised on high. The one anointed by Yaakov's God, he who lends delight to Israel's songs.

The spirit of HaShem has spoken in me; His words are on my tongue.

The God of Israel spoke, the Rock of Israel spoke to me,…a ruler over "Man"…righteous ruler…the fear of God.

...as does the morning light when the sun begins to shine, a light that is never darkened...the rain drops upon the grasses.

...my house...with God, for He has made an eternal covenant with me,...well ordered and protected...sprout forth....

But the wicked shall all be raked aside like thorns. For no one will take them in his hand.

Whoever would touch them must wear armor and provide himself with a spear. Wherever they make their home they must be burned.

It seems to me that only verse 1 provides a self-contained, self-sustaining message. Verses 2, 3 and 4 look like nothing so much as notes which a lecturer might make for himself to remind him of topics which he ought to cover. They suggest themes which could be appropriately developed, as indeed they are developed by the various commentators who suggest the additions which appear in the first version above.[1] Verses 5 and 6 are, it is true, self contained and self sustaining, but they do not appear to be heading anywhere. They seem to be more interested in the metaphor than in the subject which they are supposed to illuminate. Verse 5 does make an important point: the wicked have placed themselves beyond the pale; there can be no useful personal contact with them. However, verse 6 seems to take the *mashal* much further than is really required for the poet's purpose. Its subject seems to be the *mashal* rather than the *nimshal*. What does all this detail add to the message?

In reading the passage as it is actually written, one has the sense of peering over the shoulder of the poet as he lays out the thoughts that he plans to incorporate into his composition. In their raw state they say both too much and too little. Not all of the ideas will ultimately be used, and those that do make it to the final draft may require further embellishment.

After they will have been polished into shape—with perhaps some putative ideas rejected, others accepted, developed and perhaps augmented by associations which have not yet occurred to the poet—it will be another matter. The song will indeed have become worthy of *him who lends delight to Israel's songs*.

Let us try to discover the background against which this psalm was composed. In our examination we will have to bear in mind that, whatever the reason might be, it did not find its way into Tehilim. Why did it not? Why did Dovid never finish it?[2]

Let us soldier on and see where our efforts will take us.

Before we begin our analysis, we should probe the implications of the introductory phrase: *These are the final words of Dovid*.[3] What precisely does this mean? Radak thinks that after Dovid composed this psalm, his *ruach hakodesh*, the divine inspiration through which he wrote his other works, forsook him. This was the very last psalm which Dovid would compose.

Let us accept Radak's interpretation and follow it on to its logical conclusions. There are some questions which we need to ask. Did Dovid know that this was to be his very last composition? Did he feel his inspiration beginning to ebb? Did he intuit that nothing would ever again be the same? Did he desperately attempt to summon up reserves of his holy genius for one last mighty *tour de force*?

I do not suppose that we can ever hope to give definitive answers to these questions. I do not, if the truth be told, even know whether such questions ought to be asked. But my heart tells me that the first verse of the psalm can offer us a glimpse into Dovid's heart as he prepared himself for what may well prove itself to become the most difficult moment of his career.

Let us take a look at the verse:

The words of Dovid son of Yishay, the words of him who has been raised on high. The one anointed by Yaakov's God, he who lends delight to Israel's songs.

Why this lengthy and detailed introduction to just this psalm? Why, just here, did Dovid feel the need to describe himself so lovingly and so exhaustively? Let us examine how he introduces himself. He is: 1. Dovid son of Yishay. 2. He was taken from the sheepfolds to be suddenly raised to the dizzying heights of Israel's kingship. 3. He was anointed by Yaakov's God and 4. he was gifted with ability to lend delight to Israel's songs.

There is nothing new here, nothing that was not plainly stated or, at the very least, clearly implied in numerous passages in TaNaCh. Throughout his vast poetic output as recorded in Sefer Tehilim, a simple *Mizmor LeDovid* or the like served well as an entirely sufficient introduction which never left anybody in doubt as to who was meant or what lay concealed within that simple name. Why the sudden need for a detailed introduction?

Perhaps our earlier questions have already revealed the answer to us. Perhaps Dovid was indeed gripped by a realization that something, something very, very important, was beginning to slip away from him. Perhaps, by rehearsing to himself all those qualities which had, throughout his life, enabled him to be the unmatched singer of Israel's songs,[4] he thought that he might be able to make the supreme effort to produce one final psalm which would sum up the lessons of his tortured but exhilarating life. [5]

Did he succeed? I suspect that he did not. We noted earlier that the form in which this song has been preserved for us suggests an unfinished symphony. It is no more than a first draft, an early attempt to begin to come to grips with hazy memories of inchoate longings, a listing of suggestive nouns and phraselets which will help when the time is ripe for a true and worthy composition. As such, it certainly has no place in Sefer Tehilim.[6]

Why did Dovid never finish it? Perhaps, for the very reason which Radak revealed to us. Dovid had become the *n'im zemiros Yisrael* by virtue of the spirit which had been granted him at the moment of his investiture by Shmuel. At that exalted moment the spirit of HaShem entered him. It was while imbued by that spirit that Dovid was able to compose and shepherd to final perfection all the psalms which earned their place in Sefer Tehilim. As that spirit was about to leave him, as he felt his power ebbing, he was simply unable to find the spiritual energy required to continue and to bring his *last words* to the requisite perfection.

I wish to propose a theory. It is this. This last of all the psalms, checkered and incomplete, inspired phrases punctuated by tortured gaps, snatches of speech fizzling out into frustrated silences, is really a graphic representation of Dovid's life.[7]

I mean this in the following sense. I wish for a moment to return to the story of Dovid's investiture in I Shmuel chapter 16 verse 13. There we are told that Shmuel anointed Dovid and that, as a result, a *ru'ach HaShem*, a divine spirit, entered into him from that day onwards.[8] I am interested in that last phrase. Does it mean that the spirit was with him permanently, that throughout his life it never left him even for a moment; or does it mean that it was, so to speak, on call, waiting to be summoned for special occasions,[9] but that there were moments in Dovid's life in which he was not inspired by this spirit?

Now Rashi defines this divine spirit as a *ru'ach gevurah*, a spirit which imbued him with might. It occurred to me that if there were other places in which Rashi used this term, they might yield a clue as to whether this spirit was permanent or sporadic. My search program turned up a number of locations where Rashi renders *ru'ach HaShem* as *ru'ach gevurah*. Among them is Shoftim 14:19 where Shimshon, after the solution to his riddle had been revealed to the Philistines, was enveloped by a *ru'ach HaShem* (Rashi, = *ru'ach gevurah*), grabbed a donkey's jaw that was lying nearby, and with it killed a thousand men. The context makes it obvious that this was a one-time effort. Other examples are less clear, but taken together, certainly yield the impression that such a spirit came and went as required.

If then, this is also the case with the *ru'ach gevurah* which came upon Dovid at his investiture, we might draw the following conclusion. Just as Dovid's "final words" came to him, interrupted by gaps in which the departing spirit failed him, so his life, taken as a whole, was not one continuum of inspiration from the *ru'ach gevurah*, but there were times when he was left without the spirit and made those mistakes which ended in so much tragedy for himself and for his people.

I believe that a careful analysis of the language which TaNaCh uses may well bear out these ideas. When the divine spirit entered Dovid at his investiture (I Shmuel 16:13) TaNaCh uses *vatitzlach*.[10] Now Metzudos points out that *tzolach*[11] is synonymous with *ovar*,[12] to pass over. At II Shmuel 19:18 he makes this point more explicitly. There the verse reads, *vetzilchu HaYarden*, they *crossed* (= *ovar*) the Yarden.[13]

Now *ovar* certainly connotes a measure of temporariness. In connection with *ru'ach* the *locus classicus* is BeMidbar 5:14, where the temporary fit of jealousy which persuades the husband to ban contact between his wife and a man who has aroused his suspicions, is described as, *ve'ovar alav ru'ach kin'ah*.[14]

I think that I have made a persuasive case and believe that it has given us the key to solve a question which bears asking. It is this: what will guarantee that the Melech HaMoshiach, when he will finally come to us, will not fall into the same kind of errors which plagued the original Dovid?

I believe that a careful reading of Yeshayahu 11:2 provides the answer. There the prophet speaks of the Melech HaMoshiach and teaches us that he will be imbued with *a spirit of HaShem, a spirit of wisdom and understanding, a spirit of empathy and power, a spirit of knowledge and fear of HaShem.* Now it is true that this all seems much more than was given to Dovid at his investiture. There, only *ru'ach HaShem* is mentioned. Still, I do not believe that this is the significant change. I suppose that all the various qualities of which Yeshayahu speaks could be subsumed under *"ru'ach HaShem."* The real difference, as I understand it, lies in the verb which the prophet uses. In Yeshayahu's vision there is no *vatitzlach*, with its intimation of impermanence and punctuated experience. Instead we have *nachah*[15] from *no'ach*, to come to rest permanently as in *menuchah*.

The implication is clear and incontrovertible. The Dovid of

the future will never be without the divine spirit. There will be no room for the errors which plagued the historic Dovid.

The time has now come to think about some of those errors. As we embark upon this difficult task let us pray together with Dovid HaMelech:

גל עיני ואביטה נפלאות מתורתיך

*

*Open my eyes
So that I may behold wonders
From your Torah*

Dovid Remains in Yerushalayim

eachers have problems with the Dovid/Bas Sheva saga. Invariably, when discussions turn to the best way of teaching some of the more difficult sections of TaNaCh, this story is brought up as a prime problem. How do we present it to our students without somehow undermining the standing of Dovid HaMelech in their eyes?

The question is reasonable, but there are answers. Let us sit down together and approach this *sugia* as we would any other in the Torah. An earnest analysis of the relevant texts together with the profound insights with which Chazal and our *Chachmei HaMesorah* have gifted us, will see us through.

Instead of treating this incident in isolation, we will approach it with an eye to the context in which TaNaCh presents it to us. Much about what happened can be illumined by studying the passages that border on the story.

On our journey of discovery, we will venture far beyond the account in Shmuel. To get the full flavor of the role that this unfortunate incident played in Dovid's life, we must augment the Shmuel account with that of Divrei HaYamim. Now cognoscenti will smile at this statement because, in fact, Divrei HaYamim ignores the entire incident; it is simply not mentioned. Nevertheless, I stand by my assertion. There are different ways of ignoring things and I believe that Divrei HaYamim has chosen a way for itself that is fraught with significant implications.

So let us start at what ought really to be the end of a logically structured presentation. Let us look at the absence of this story in I Divrei HaYamim 20:1–2.

א.   ויהי לעת תשובת השנה לעת צאת המלכים וינהג יואב את חיל הצבא
וישחת את ארץ בני עמון ויבא ויצר את רבה ודויד ישב בירושלם ויך יואב
את רבה ויהרסה.

ב.   ויקח דויד את עטרת מלכם מעל ראשו וימצאה משקל ככר זהב ובה
אבן יקרה ותהי על ראש דויד ושלל העיר הוציא הרבה מאד.

1.   Now, as the year moved toward a new beginning, at a time of the year when kings would go out to war, Yoav commandeered the army and destroyed the land of the Ammonites. He went on to besiege Rabbah while Dovid stayed in Yerushalayim. Yoav smote Rabbah and destroyed it.

2.   Dovid removed the [Ammonite] king's crown from his head and found it to weigh as much as a kikar of gold. It had a precious stone embedded in it. Henceforth it would be on Dovid's head. He took exceedingly abundant spoils from the city.

These two verses do not fit well together. The first tells us that as the city was being sacked, Dovid was staying in Yerushalayim. How, then, was he able to remove the crown from the head of the Moabite king as reported in verse 2?

The discord between the two verses is so jarring that we instinctively feel that something must be missing between them. We will find that indeed there is. A full fifty-five verses have, so to speak, gone *awol*.

To understand what happened, we will need to locate the parallel verses in the Shmuel account. Our verse 1 parallels II Shmuel 11:1. Our verse 2 parallels II Shmuel 12:30. Fifty-five verses separate the two. Those verses tell the entire story of Dovid and Bas Sheva and also provide much additional material concerning Yoav's campaign against Ammon. The information contained in those buffer verses completely eliminates the problem that the Divrei HaYamim passage posed for us.

However, the fact remains that these verses are missing from Divrei HaYamim. The Chronicler seems to have set us a challenge. He combines two verses that cannot be reconciled without additional information—but he withholds that information. What was his thinking? How does he want us to react to the conundrum with which he confronts us?

The series of essays we intend to devote to Dovid and Bas Sheva will not deal with the question of why Divrei HaYamim chooses to ignore that story. The answer to this problem belongs in an examination of the Chronicler's motivation for writing an account that, essentially, covers the same ground as II Shmuel and I and II Melachim. The task of such an analysis will be to explain why, in spite of very broad agreement concerning what belongs in such an account, there are still many parts of the earlier books that the Chronicler omits and there are many other passages that he includes although they do not appear in the earlier books. Such an analysis is of course vastly important, but it is not a part of the Dovidic saga that is the focus of the present book.[1]

However, the material about the campaign against the Ammonites that Shmuel treats in detail while Divrei HaYamim mentions only in passing, does very much fall within the ambit of our interest. You, dear reader, will soon discover why.

It is now time to offer our analysis of how the two books treat Yoav's Ammonite campaign.

In II Shmuel, the story begins at 11:1 where we are told that Dovid sent Yoav to attack the Ammonites; that Yoav wrought destruction upon Ammon; and that, while Dovid stayed in Yerushalayim, Yoav laid siege upon Ammon's capital city, Rabbah.

After that introductory verse, following upon the statement that Dovid uncharacteristically had stayed in Yerushalayim, the story of Dovid and Bas Sheva begins to unfold. It continues until II Shmuel 12:26, where the Ammonite campaign is once again picked up. In verses 26–28 we have the loyal Yoav sending a message to Dovid that he is ready to invade Rabbah, but that he suggests that Dovid should join him so that the honor of capturing the city should accrue to the king rather than to Yoav. Verse 29 then tells us that Dovid followed Yoav's advice, made his way to Ammon, and captured the city. Verse 30, which parallels the second Divrei HaYamim verse, then tells how Dovid took the crown of the Ammonite king.

Everything in the Shmuel account is perfectly logical and there is nothing of the difficulty we had with the Divrei HaYamim passage.

Now, had the Chronicler so desired, he had a number of options available to him to avoid placing two contradictory verses next to each other. In the earlier verse he could have left out the information that Dovid stayed in Yerushalayim. That was a necessary piece of information in the Shmuel account where it serves as an introduction to the Bas Sheva story. The Chronicler did not intend to tell that story and could have left out that piece of information, without apparent loss to his purpose.

If for some reason he felt that this information was too important to ignore, he could have mentioned Yoav's invitation to Dovid and recorded that Dovid accepted that invitation and joined Yoav in Ammon. Again, the problem would have been eliminated.

He could also have left out the story of Dovid removing the Ammonite king's crown and placing it on his own head.

Each of these three options could have eliminated the problem we raised. However, he took none of them but placed the two, really unconnected verses in direct juxtaposition to each other, leaving us with a vexing conundrum: why?

There is more. We know from the Shmuel account what motivated Yoav to send for Dovid. It was a gesture of loyalty, a willingness on the part of a general to remain out of the limelight and allow his king to take the credit for the sacking of Ammon's capital city. Indeed, the account we have in Shmuel precisely reflects Yoav's intention. It is Dovid who delivers the coup de grâce and captures Rabbah, precisely as loyal Yoav had planned it.

In the Divrei HaYamim passage we quoted above, things look very different. Immediately after the *pasuk* tells us that Dovid had remained in Yerushalayim during the crucial campaign, it goes on to say, *Yoav smote Rabbah and destroyed it.* There is no mention at all of Dovid.

The same excision of Dovid's involvement is just as evident earlier, in verse 1. Where the Shmuel account mentions that it was Dovid who sent Yoav on his way, Divrei HaYamim has nothing of this. It is Yoav who, apparently on his own initiative, *commandeered the army and destroyed the land of the Ammonites.*

All this indicates that by the time of Ezra, who wrote Divrei

HaYamim, the folk memory of these events took the precise form that Yoav in his loyalty to Dovid had sought to avoid. The honor of the victory accrued not to Dovid but to Yoav!

We may sum up our findings so far as follows: The Chronicler had his own reasons for not wishing to include the Dovid/Bas Sheva story in his history. Nevertheless, he would not forego the opportunity of noting his criticism of Dovid HaMelech's bearing in this whole matter.

He accomplished this by taking the following steps.

1. He records—unnecessarily since he will not tell the story of Bas Sheva—that Dovid had remained in Yerushalayim during Yoav's Ammonite campaign.
2. He tells how Dovid took the crown from the Ammonite king without having mentioned Yoav's invitation and Dovid's acquiescence. By doing so he confronts us with a problem and, so to speak, forces us back to the Shmuel account where we will learn of the Dovid/Bas Sheva saga and also that Yoav's plan had been that the glory of the conquest should accrue to Dovid.
3. Having thus obliquely informed us of all this, he does precisely what Yoav, in his loyalty, had tried to avoid. He ascribes the honor to Yoav and denies the king the glory that, so we learn in Shmuel, should rightly have been his.

As a result of these stratagems, the Chronicler succeeds in placing Dovid in a very negative light.

Was he right? Should Dovid really be faulted for his passivity during the Ammonite campaign?

Why did Dovid stay in Yerushalayim? Let us spend just a few moments examining this issue before we go on to the next chapter.

Jewish kings do not stay in the comfort of their capital city while their armies go out and fight. When the people asked Shmuel to anoint a king for them they mentioned expressly that part of this monarch's duty would be that HE WILL GO OUT IN FRONT OF US *and wage our wars* (I Shmuel 8:20). Later, in II Shmuel 21:17, where some of the Philistine wars are described, the people, afraid for Dovid's safety, actually swore that henceforth they would not allow the elderly king to come to the front. Clearly it was Dovid's custom to be present in the thickest midst of the battles his armies fought.

Dovid was certainly not one to shirk battle.

Why, then, did Dovid, against all precedent, remain in Yerushalayim during this significant campaign? Why did fate conspire that, although he eventually made his way to the front at Yoav's urging, that gesture would be forgotten and the honor of the victory would be denied him?

We have solved a number of textual problems but, in the end, have only deepened the mystery.

Come! We have much to learn.

An Ill-fated Gesture of Kindness

hy did Dovid stay in Yerushalayim during the Ammonite campaign? The question rankles so, because such an apparent shrugging off of responsibility is so hugely out of character. Everything that we know about Dovid HaMelech militates against such an irresponsible abdication of duty toward his people and his soldiers.

The fact that both Shmuel and Divrei HaYamim make a point of mentioning this apparent dereliction shows that it was regarded as a very serious matter. So why not help us along by providing a clue, at the very least as to what might have persuaded Dovid that in this situation, passivity was the route to follow?

The question seems so reasonable that, really, it admits of only one answer. It must be that, indeed, an explanation lies at hand. To spot it requires only that we widen our perspective and, as we promised earlier, look outside the story itself for relevant material. Let us explore the neighborhood in which the action takes place and see what we can find.

The story of Dovid and Bas Sheva is told in II Shmuel, chapter 11. I would like to examine what happened in the chapter immediately preceding that one. Here is how it begins.

ויהי אחרי כן וימת מלך בני עמון וימלך חנון בנו תחתיו. ויאמר דוד אעשה
חסד עם חנון בן נחש כאשר עשה אביו עמדי חסד וישלח דוד לנחמו ביד
עבדיו אל אביו ויבאו עבדי דוד ארץ בני עמון.

After that, the king of the Ammonites died and his son, Chonun, became king in his stead.

Dovid said, "Let me do a kindness to Chonun son of Nachash just as his father did a kindness to me.[1] So Dovid sent a delegation made up of his servants to comfort him for the loss of his father.[2] His servants arrived in the land of the Ammonites.

As we go along in our analysis we will learn how this seemingly innocent gesture led to stark tragedy. It turns out that good instincts do not always lead in the right direction. Let us trace what happened.

Here is a quote from Midrash Rabbah BeMidbar 21:5. It refers to the nations of Ammon and Moav.

"אע"פ שכתבתי 'כי תקרב אל עיר להלחם אליה וקראת אליה לשלום' לאלו לא תעשו כן. 'לא תדרוש שלומם וטובתם.'" את מוצא במי שבא עמהם במדת רחמים לסוף בא לידי בזיון מלחמות [וצרות] ואיזה זה דוד. ויאמר דוד, "אעשה חסד עם חנון בן נחש." אמר לו הקב"ה, "אתה תעבור על דברי אני כתבתי 'לא תדרוש שלומם וטובתם' ואתה עושה עמם גמילות חסד? אל תהי צדיק הרבה!" שלא יהא אדם מוותר על התורה.

[God spoke:] "Even though I wrote [in my Torah] *When you approach a city to wage war against it, you shall first offer them peace,* in the case of these two nations you are not to do so. You are not to care for their benefit or well-being. Our experience shows that if you approach them with gestures of mercy, in the end it will bring war and all manner of suffering. Dovid is an example of this, for Dovid said, "Let me do kindness...." So God said to him, "You are flouting My wishes. I wrote that you are not to seek out *their benefit or their well-being* and you show him kindness? Do not be more of a *tzadik* than is required of you! Let no man be careless concerning the Torah's prescriptions.

That sounds very harsh. Was there nothing to justify Dovid? He cannot simply have cavalierly ignored the Torah's strictures. So there must have been a rationalization. Did it work? Was it a good one? Was it solid? If it was weak, why would Dovid have relied upon it? If it was strong, why does the midrash castigate him?

One way of explaining Dovid's decision is to postulate that the Torah's prohibition against showing kindness to Ammon and Moav is limited to situations in which a Jew wants to do them a favor out of the goodness of his heart. He likes them and wants to show it. That is precisely what the Torah forbids. Dovid's case, however, does not fit into that paradigm. He rea-

soned that he had a moral obligation to show consideration
for the Ammonite king. He was not following the dictates of
a misplaced love, but fulfilling what he conceived to be a duty.
He may well have concluded that such a gesture would not be
interdicted (see Kesef Mishneh, Hilchos Melachim 6:6).

There are other ideas that may have persuaded Dovid of
the correctness of his actions.

A glance at the Rambam where he codifies the prohibition
against seeking out the benefit and well-being of Ammon and
Moav (Melachim 6:6) will suggest just such a possibility.

עמון ומואב אין שולחין להם לשלום שנאמר לא תדרוש שלומם וטובתם
כל ימיך אמרו חכמים לפי שנאמר וקראת אליה לשלום יכול עמון ומואב
כן תלמוד לומר לא תדרוש שלומם וטובתם לפי שנאמר עמך ישב בקרבך
בטוב לו לא תוננו יכול עמון ומואב כן תלמוד לומר וטובתם....

No peaceful overtures may be made to Ammon and
Moav [before waging war against them] for it is written,
*Do not, throughout your history, seek out their benefit or
their well-being*...Furthermore since it is written [about
a *Ger Toshav*, a non-Jew who has formally undertaken
to abide by the Noachide laws], *He may dwell among you,
in your very midst, such that it should be good for him. Do
not inflict suffering upon him,* it might have appeared that
this dispensation applies even to [a *Ger Toshav*] from
Ammon and Moav, therefore it says *[Do not seek out]
their benefit....*

Rambam's formulation indicates that the prohibition is addressed to the community rather than to the individual. Both
the obligation to make peaceful overtures before waging war
and the dispensation of permitting a *Ger Toshav* to live among
us in Eretz Yisrael are matters of the public, not the private,
domain.

Thus may Dovid have rationalized. He sent the messengers as an individual who appreciated a favor once done to his
family (see note 1); it had nothing to do with his kingly duties
and therefore did not fall within the public domain.

Either of these explanations seems reasonable enough. Why, then, could these considerations not have exonerated Dovid from the midrash's stricture?[3]

It seems to me that the answer must lie with a principle established by my good friend R. Yehudah Coperman in one of his important studies of the function of *p'shat* where the simple meaning of the text does not accord with the *halachah*. He suggests that in such a situation the *p'shat* may be teaching us what is desirable rather than that which is obligatory.[4]

Here is an example where we see this principle applied.

In chapter 36 of BeMidbar we learn that God commanded the daughters of Tzelaphchad to choose a husband from within their tribe so that the inheritance that they would receive through their late father would not pass to a different tribe upon their death. Now the simple reading of that *parashah* yields that this requirement would be applicable to all women, always. Nevertheless, Chazal interpret a certain word in the *parashah* in such a way that, for practical purposes, only women from that generation were interdicted from marrying out of their own tribe.

Now, in Shoftim 11:1, we learn that Yiphtach, one of the Judges, was the son of a *zonah*, a loose woman. The Targum explains that the mother was not an actual harlot but that people looked upon her as a *zonah* because she had married out of her own tribe. It was customary in those times that a woman who acted thus would be known as a *zonah*.

Clearly then, although, as we noted above, the *halachah* did not forbid such a union for women who were not part of the first generation in the wilderness, the usage nevertheless met with opprobrium to the extent that women who made use of the license to marry out were known as loose women.

We can use the same principle to understand how Dovid could have been faulted for doing what the *halachah* clearly permitted. Although what he did was not included within the Torah's interdiction, still the simple meaning of the text does not make that clear. Read simply, it would seem that any kindness shown to Ammon and Moav would be displeasing to the Ribono shel Olam. It is true that Dovid did not flout the *halachah* but he should still not have done what he did. The Torah makes clear that even what is not formally prohibited is nevertheless to be avoided.

As the midrash points out, Dovid's gesture led to tragedy. The story goes on to tell how Chonun's ministers persuaded him that the avowed purpose of the delegation, that they had come to comfort him, was really only a cover for their real intentions; they had come to spy out the land. Chonun allowed himself to be convinced and subjected Dovid's messengers to extreme humiliation. Before he sent them on their way, he cut off half their beards and half their clothes, leaving the lower parts of their bodies naked.

Dovid felt that he had to avenge this insult and sent his armies out to fight against Ammon. Dovid's forces were victorious in the ensuing battles. This brings us to the end of chapter 10. Chapter 11, the one that has been the focus of our interest because it tells the story of Dovid and Bas Sheva, begins with the information that Dovid ordered Yoav to take an army to attack the Ammonites in their own country. It is this battle that we discussed in the previous chapter. It is the battle concerning which TaNaCh tells us that Dovid elected to remain in Yerushalayim.

From all that we have now learned, it seems quite obvious why Dovid felt that it would be inappropriate to take part in the battle for Ammon. War is always a tragedy and the lives lost can never be recovered. Dovid must have realized that but for his ill-conceived idea to send the delegation to Chonun, none of this suffering need have happened. Weighed down by his guilt, he felt that he had best not be involved in the fighting.

We have fulfilled our promise to look outside the actual *parashah* of Dovid and Bas Sheva for the background against which all that happened took place. We are now ready, with much care and the requisite earnestness, to begin our analysis of that sad story.

Dovid's State of Mind Made Him Prone to Error

ow did Dovid feel whiling away his time in Yerushalayim, knowing all along that he really belonged among his troops on the battlefields of Ammon? Of course, we cannot really know. Nevertheless, Chazal can guide us toward some reasonable thinking. Here is a passage from Sanhedrin 107a.

אמר רב יהודה אמר רב לעולם אל יביא אדם עצמו לידי נסיון שהרי דוד מלך ישראל הביא עצמו לידי נסיון ונכשל אמר לפניו רבונו של עולם מפני מה אומרים אלהי אברהם אלהי יצחק ואלהי יעקב ואין אומרים אלהי דוד אמר אינהו מינסו לי ואת לא מינסית לי אמר לפניו רבונו של עולם בחנני ונסני שנאמר בחנני ה' ונסני וגו' אמר מינסנא לך ועבידנא מילתא בהדך דלדידהו לא הודעתינהו ואילו אנא קא מודענא לך דמנסינא לך בדבר ערוה מיד ויהי לעת הערב ויקם דוד מעל משכבו וגו' אמר רב יהודה שהפך משכבו של לילה למשכבו של יום ונתעלמה ממנו הלכה אבר קטן יש באדם משביעו רעב ומרעיבו שבע.

R. Yehudah taught in the name of Rav. Never ask for your piety to be tested. For Dovid, King of Israel, asked to be tested and failed.

[Here is what happened.]

Dovid asked God, "Why were You described as the 'God of Avraham, Yitzchak, and Yaakov' but never as the 'God of Dovid'"?

God answered, "These three proved themselves in various tests; you were never tested."

Dovid pleaded, "Test me so that I will be able to prove my mettle."

God answered, "I will test you and I will even let you know the area in which you will be tested. The test will involve forbidden relationships."

Immediately upon this conversation, we learn that, *"Now it was toward evening that Dovid rose from his bed…"* R. Yehudah taught that this verse informs us that Dovid did by day what should only be done at night (he indulged in conjugal relationship with one of his wives).

He had forgotten the teaching that *man has a small limb;
if he satiates it, its craving increases, but if he starves it, it will
be satisfied.*

I have learned this piece of Gemara many times, but have
never before asked myself whether there is any indication at
what stage of his life Dovid began to wonder why he had been
denied what had been granted to the patriarchs.

It struck me, though I cannot claim to have even a scin-
tilla of proof for my thesis, that the question may well have
occurred to Dovid while he was in Yerushalayim during the
Ammonite campaign. My reasoning is as follows.

Before we can hazard even a guess, we need to examine
more closely what qualities are required so that a person would
merit that the name of God would be associated with his. We
might phrase this same question a little differently. How did
Dovid understand that of all the great people who ever lived,
only the Avos, not even, let us say, Moshe Rabbeinu, were
gifted with this great merit? Moreover, what made him think
that he, more than anybody else, shared with them whatever
quality it was that made them special?

For an explanation, we will go to Maharal in his Chidushei
Aggada to Sanhedrin. He explains that God will allow His
name to be associated only with a communal entity, not
with an individual. The Avos *qua* Avos, and only they, were
communal entities.[1] Each one of them was, so to speak, Klal
Yisrael incarnate. No one, not even Moshe Rabbeinu, could
lay claim to such a status.[2]

Dovid based his case that he deserved the same treatment
as the Avos upon his view of the kingship and of his personal
relationship to it. He argued that if an "Av," as an "Av," is a communal figure rather than an individual, then so is he. His relationship to all the subsequent kings was that of an "Av" since
they would all descend from him and would draw their royal
privileges from his *ur*-kingship. Furthermore, the kingship by
its very nature is a communal institution since the ruler carries the entire people within his heart.[3]

That given, we may surmise that the time that he was staying in Yerushalayim would have been a time in which this question plagued him in a particularly painful manner. He wondered whether his failure to be at the front together with his troops did not throw a pall over his claim to be a public figure in the same sense that the Avos were. If, indeed, his personality was to be defined solely in terms of the people over whom he ruled, should he not now have been on the battlefield together with them? Perhaps by staying in Yerushalayim he had made a statement. Perhaps by his own inaction he had shown that he had no right to the status that he claimed.

As his conscience would not let him rest, he may well have craved reassurance. Had he betrayed the essence of his kingship? He turns to God and poses the dread question. What will the Ribono shel Olam answer him?

He must have felt relief when the Ribono shel Olam did not refute the entire basis upon which he had staked his claim. It seemed from the answer he received that, if he would but overcome the hurdle by which the Ribono shel Olam would test him, he would indeed, on the strength of his kingship, equal the public persona of the Avos; the expression "God of Dovid" would become as natural as "God of Avraham, Yitzchak, and Yaakov."

The test would be the key to his vindication. He would not have to plague himself with the dreadful thought that his ill-conceived gesture in sending the delegation to Chonun, or even the tragic aftermath to which it gave rise, had permanently scarred his kingship. All was well, or at least, all could be well, if he would but be strong when the decisive moment came.

It is easy to see that, with so much at stake, Dovid would have given less thought than usual to the more theoretical issue of whether or not one ought to stalk *nisyonos*. He needed desperately to find out where he now stood.

Nevertheless, desperation is not a frame of mind that encourages straight thinking. His eagerness to be tested was in error. Error breeds error and it would not be long before Dovid would make another mistake.

Now it was toward evening that Dovid rose from his bed.

Chazal, in the passage that we quoted above, read much into this seemingly innocent description. As they interpret it, Dovid, knowing that he was to face a test in physical self-control, was attempting to guarantee himself mastery over his natural urges. He engaged in marital relations as much as possible, that is, even when inappropriate such as during the day, hoping thereby to lessen his desires when the test would be upon him.

As we see in the passage quoted above, Chazal fault him for this decision. He should have remembered that excessive use stimulates the "small limb" and that only abstinence can satiate it. However, even if we were to take the text in its more simple meaning, if Dovid would just have been taking an afternoon nap, there is still something disconcerting about it. We recall Rashi to Shemos 17:11, who teaches that, in the battle against Amalek, Moshe Rabbeinu rested on a stone rather than upon a cushion because he was determined to eschew comfort while his people were in the throes of battle. With this in mind, it is hard to understand why Dovid should have pampered himself by sleeping in the afternoon, when his army was out on the battlefield.

Clearly—and understandably—Dovid was not himself. His ultimate failing of the test was of a piece with the other errors he had made. We will leave that sad story to the next chapter.

An Afternoon Stroll

ויתהלך על גג בית המלך וירא אשה רוחצת מעל הגג והאשה טובת מראה
מאד בת שבע הוה קא חייפא רישא תותי חלתא אתא שטן אידמי ליה
כציפרתא פתק ביה גירא פתקה לחלתא איגליה וחזייה מיד וישלח דוד
וידרוש לאשה ויאמר הלא זאת בת שבע בת אליעם אשת אוריה החתי
וישלח דוד מלאכים ויקחה ותבא אליו וישכב עמה והיא מתקדשת
מטומאתה ותשב אל ביתה.

Dovid was strolling around on the palace roof, when he
spotted a woman of exceptional beauty washing herself.

Bas Sheva had been washing her hair, protected by
a screen [lit. a beehive]. The Satan [intent upon causing mischief] disguised himself as a bird [knowing that
Dovid would feel himself challenged to shoot at it].
Dovid shot an arrow at the bird and [missing its target]
it pierced the screen. Bas Sheva was thus exposed and
Dovid saw her. He sent a messenger [to find out her
identity] and learned that she was Bas Sheva, daughter
of Eliam and wife of Uriah the Hittite. Dovid sent for
her. She came to him and he lay with her, she having pu-
rified herself from any defilement. She then returned
home.

(Sanhedrin 107a)

*T*his story is preposterous by any standard. We are
talking of the great and holy[1] Dovid HaMelech,
sweet singer of Israel's psalms, progenitor of the
Melech HaMoshiach. Would such a one sink so low?
Could such a one sink so low? Can we imagine any *ehrlicher
yid* of just normal decency, even thinking of doing what he
did? We will have to dig a little deeper to make sense of it all.

We note in passing that Maharal (Chidushei Aggada to
Sanhedrin, there) reads the passage as an allegory. We will
take a quick glance at what Maharal says because it comports
well with our theory that Dovid was not himself during this
entire episode.

Maharal sees the beehive as a metaphor for the Torah. Here

is how. A beehive contains that which is sweet—the honey, and that which stings—the bees. In that sense, it is like the Torah that showers us with happiness if we walk in its ways, and punishes us painfully if we do not. In the metaphor, the beehive protected Bas Sheva from prying eyes in precisely the same way that the Torah protects us from inappropriate desires. The "beehive" sheltered Bas Sheva from Dovid's interest and, before the Satan interfered, everything was as it should have been.

Satan decides to intervene. For his plans, he needs to appear to Dovid as a bird that Dovid will want to hunt. Maharal explains: People enjoy hunting. It is a pleasurable form of relaxation for its acolytes. That given, it serves well as an allegory for a leisure activity, one that does not demand much from us.[2] It is the precise opposite of the all-encompassing, unbending concentration required for immersion in Torah study. When the narrator tells us that Dovid saw a bird and tried to shoot it, he is conveying the idea that to a degree Dovid was shrugging off the yoke of Torah, preferring a looser, more forgiving activity to his general disciplined immersion in learning.

Conceived thus, the arrow—physical metaphor for the tools we all find to free ourselves occasionally from the tensions of uninterrupted concentration upon Torah studies—will indeed smash the protective beehive that is Torah. Bereft of the safeguard that Torah provides, Dovid was defenseless before the attraction of Bas Sheva's beauty.

If this is indeed what happened, then such an out-of-character attenuation of his commitment to Torah, that which Dovid himself had described as his most pleasurable activity,[3] as that which filled his life with music,[4] can only be seen as of a piece with the depressed mood that made possible the series of mistakes that preceded it.

Maharal does indeed comport well with the thesis that we have been developing in the last few chapters.

Now let us see what happens if we take the story at face value; if the arrow and the beehive were indeed nothing more than an arrow and a beehive. How can we unravel the many mysteries that make up this story?

We have already wondered at the strange picture of Dovid taking a stroll on the palace roof when he rose from his afternoon nap. That is only the beginning. Can we imagine a Gadol BeYisrael feeling the urge to take a shot at a passing bird? What could have made Dovid HaMelech want to do that? Moreover, since it is Dovid the consummate warrior who is doing the shooting, can it really be that, once committed to this apparently senseless act, he would miss? He had no difficulty landing the stone that killed Golias precisely where he wanted it. Suddenly we are faced with a Dovid who not only makes halachic and hashkafic errors but is also an inept sharpshooter!

There is more. What did Dovid make of the fact that of all the places at which the arrow might have landed, of all the times at which the incident might have occurred, it went unerringly to the precise place, and was timed unerringly to the precise moment, that would reveal Bas Sheva to him?

Let us learn a little more.

ראויה היתה בת שבע בת אליעם לדוד מששת ימי בראשית אלא שבאה אליו במכאוב וכן תנא דבי רבי ישמעאל ראויה היתה לדוד בת שבע בת אליעם אלא שאכלה פגה.

Bas Sheva had been earmarked to become Dovid's wife from the very moment when the world was created. [If he had not erred, his union with her would have come about painlessly. Because of what he did] it came about through pain. So too did they teach in the Yeshiva of R. Yishmael: Bas Sheva had indeed been earmarked for Dovid. However, [he took her before the appropriate time. He was] as one who eats a grape before it ripened.

This *sugia* certainly provides a key to what is perhaps the greatest mystery in this difficult story. Is it possible that Dovid would want to lie with a strange woman simply because she was beautiful? The place that Dovid HaMelech plays in Jewish tradition and Jewish thinking tells us that this is simply not possible.

Armed with the profound insight that Chazal offer us here,

the matter becomes much less problematic. As the protective screen burst open, Dovid experienced an epiphany. Here was a soul mate, one whom the Ribono shel Olam had surely determined to be his wife from the very dawn of history.[5] He knew with great certainty that his life was about to find fulfillment, that here was the woman who would gift him with immortality since it was by her, and by no one else, that Shlomo and the Messianic line were to be brought into the world.

We are now ready to return to our earlier question. How did Dovid explain to himself that his quite ordinary arrow, sent on its way during an unremarkable afternoon stroll on the palace roof, chose that particular target at that particular moment to bring him face-to-face with his destiny?

Let us dignify our attempted explanation with a chapter of its own. It is an important key to much that has so troubled us. Come, let us learn.

SIXTEEN

Strange Encounters

*W*e ended the previous chapter by wondering how Dovid perceived the strange sequence of events that had led to the destiny-packed moment when he came face-to-face with Bas Sheva. What a strange afternoon it had been! He had lain down for a nap, perhaps had even been intimate with one of his wives, apparently unperturbed by the terrible dangers and fears to which his soldiers, battling on Ammonite turf, were at that very moment exposed. He woke, apparently unrefreshed, so that he felt the need to take the air on the palace roof. His mood seems to have been somehow shiftless and rootless, unable, perhaps unmotivated, to turn to his first love, the study of Torah. He seeks diversion in the relaxing pleasure of the hunt—surely, one supposes, an unusual pastime for the sweet singer of Israel's songs[1]—and then, probably against all prior experience, misses his quarry.

The arrow does not let him rest. Instead of simply falling wherever gravity directs, it forges on and wreaks havoc with his life. Not an inch to the right or to the left, not a second too soon or too late, it flies inexorably on and lands squarely at the very fulcrum of his fate.

What did it all mean?

It is not hard to imagine the thoughts that must have coursed through Dovid's mind at the pivotal moment at which he suddenly came face-to-face with his destiny. He had been told that he was to be tested. He knew that the test was to involve a questionable relationship with a woman. He must certainly have suspected that the moment of challenge was now upon him. However, he was in a quandary: what would be considered passing the test? What was he to do? Should he take some action or was he expected to remain passive? Was he to read the obviously ordained path of the arrow's flight as a mandate to take Bas Sheva—in spite of the distasteful circumstances[2] that made that act so fraught with ambiguity—or was he to remain uninvolved even though that would entail turning his back on the sign the Ribono shel Olam had so obviously sent him?

There is another point that must have made him wonder. Which of his personae was being tested? Was it Dovid the man, an individual struggling with his own devils, or was it Dovid the king, a public figure, guardian of the monarchy and progenitor of the King Messiah? It was eminently possible that what was correct for the one would be considered failure for the other. How was he to know?

It is likely that he concluded that it was as king, not as an individual, that he was being tested. This is so because, as we recall from chapter 14, it was in his capacity as the "father" of royalty in Israel that he had staked his claim that the name of the Ribono shel Olam should be associated with him. This argument was never refuted. G-d did not say that his logic was faulty, only that he would first have to be tested. It seems likely that Dovid would have assumed that he was being tried in his capacity as king.

Once that was established, Dovid did not lack models for the difficult situation in which he found himself. He could look back to Yehudah who, on one occasion, found himself entangled with a "prostitute" and fathered twins from her. Then there was Boaz, who woke up one night to find a woman lying at his feet and needed to make some difficult[3] decisions. With these precedents in mind, Dovid may well have concluded that such confusing encounters were, for some reason, the norm for the key figures in the establishment of the monarchy.[4] It must have seemed logical to view his present predicament as a part of that continuum.

Once these connections were established in his mind, the decisions he made would certainly have seemed to him to be perfectly reasonable. The analysis of why this conclusion was in error and the determination of what really lay behind the earlier experiences of Dovid's forebears deserve a chapter of their own. Come with me, dear reader. We have much to do.

Yehudah and Tamar I

*D*id Dovid, at that pivotal moment when the errant arrow crashed through the screen, allow his thoughts to flash back to Yehudah and Boaz? Did it occur to him that, very likely, Bas Sheva was *his* "Tamar" in precisely the same way that Rus had apparently been the "Tamar" who put Boaz to *his* test? In the previous chapter, we suggested just that. I do not know of a Chazal that makes the connection, but it seems likely enough that this is precisely what happened. Let us continue on this assumption. As long as we know that it is no more than a plausible suggestion, we are on safe ground.

The time has come to think about Yehudah and Tamar.

I admit to being in a quandary, one that I would like to share with you, dear reader. Those of you who have accompanied me on my journeys through some of the other books in this series will know that I enjoy using Rashi and Ramban to reach beneath the surface of those sections of TaNaCh that are relevant to the particular subject that is before us. In the present instance, that reasonable method does not work so well. The Torah's account of the Yehudah and Tamar saga presents us with a difficulty that Ramban appears to ignore completely, while Rashi's treatment appears to me to fall short of offering complete satisfaction.

Here is the problem. The beginning of *parashas* VaYeishev tells the story of Yosef's dreams and describes how he subsequently fell into his brothers' hands. It takes the story to the point at which these sell him to a group of merchants who were on their way to Egypt. This section ends at Bereishis 37:36, which reads, *The Medanim sold him in[1] Egypt, to Pharaoh's minister, the chief butcher.* At this point, the story of Yehudah and Tamar begins. It runs from Bereishis 38:1 until the last verse of chapter 38. This is followed by Bereishis 39:1, *Now Yosef was taken down to Egypt where Potiphar, Pharaoh's minister, the chief butcher who was an Egyptian citizen, bought him from the Ishmaelites who had brought him down to Egypt.* Now this is information we already know from Bereishis 37:36. Rashi explains that it is repeated here only to act as a bridge to the earlier account and to lead us into the remainder of Yosef's story. From this point we hear nothing more about Yehudah and Tamar.

The problem is obvious enough. Why insert the story of Yehudah and Tamar in the middle of the Yosef saga? I have not been able to find any reference to this issue in the Ramban although it is a fact that throughout his commentary he deals frequently—as far as I know, much more frequently than does Rashi—with *parashiyos* that appear in unexpected places.

Rashi does raise the issue and suggests two explanations. The first is at Bereishis 38:1.

> Why was this *parashah* [that of Yehudah and Tamar] written here, interrupting the Yosef saga in the middle? It is in order to teach us that the brothers deposed[2] Yehudah from his high office when they saw Yaakov suffering because of Yosef's supposed death. The brothers said, "It was your idea to sell him. Had you proposed to send him back to Yaakov, we would have listened to you."

The second Rashi is at Bereishis 39:1, where the Yosef saga is picked up once more. There Rashi says:

> At this point, we go back to the earlier story. It was interrupted only in order that Yehudah's downward movement should be juxtaposed to the story of the sale of Yosef, to let us know that it was because of the sale that he was demoted. Then there is another reason. The Torah wanted to put the story of Yosef's struggle with Potiphar's wife next to the story of Tamar inveigling Yehudah to be with her. This is to teach us that just as Tamar's motivation was "for the sake of heaven" so too, the wife of Potiphar did what she did "for the sake of heaven."

There are technical issues with Rashi's approach,[3] but these need not detain us here. I am more concerned with the following thought. Both the explanations that Rashi offers provide rationalizations that, although in Rashi's mind apparently adequate, do not deal with the *parashah* of Yehudah and Tamar *qua parashah*. We are left with the feeling that, from the point of view of the story itself, it would have done better had it been placed somewhere else. It was put here as a commentary on two issues that lie entirely outside itself. We now know that Yehudah trusted his brothers too little and that Potiphar's wife acted "for the sake of heaven." Neither of these pieces of information affects the story of Yehudah and Tamar in the slightest.

Would Rashi not have done better had he produced an explanation that would have shown that this location, and no other, was the ideal venue for telling us the story of Yehudah and Tamar? Had he looked for one, he could easily have found it in a midrash that we will quote immediately. I am at a loss to understand why Rashi chose to ignore this Chazal. It seems to me that it would have provided us with an explanation that is much more satisfying than the ones Rashi offers.

Here is the midrash.

רבי שמואל בר נחמן פתח (ירמיה כט) כי אנכי ידעתי את המחשבות,
שבטים היו עסוקין במכירתו של יוסף ויוסף היה עסוק בשקו ובתעניתו
ראובן היה עסוק בשקו ובתעניתו ויעקב היה עסוק בשקו ובתעניתו ויהודה
היה עסוק ליקח לו אשה והקב"ה היה עוסק בורא אורו של מלך המשיח.

R. Shmuel bar Nachman opened a homily on Yirmiyahu 29:11 as follows: *For I know the thoughts...*[4] [at the time when the story of Yehudah and Tamar took place] Yosef's brothers were busy selling him to Egypt; Yosef himself was in mourning; Reuven was in mourning; Yaakov was in mourning; and Yehudah was looking for a wife. [while all these people were occupied with their own concerns] the Ribono shel Olam was busy creating the "light" of the Moshiach.

We are immediately struck by the sheer rightness of inserting the Yehudah and Tamar saga at this particular place, in the middle of the Yosef narrative. To the extent that it describes for us the first blossoming of the royal line[5] that will culminate in the Melech HaMoshiach, it belongs here and nowhere else. Yosef had just been brought to Egypt and sold into slavery. It was the moment in Jewish history when the very first Jew was dragged into the very first exile. It was the moment when the seed of ultimate redemption had to be planted. None of the main actors among the small family that at that time consti-tuted the Jewish people had any idea of the implications. Not troubled by any qualms, they were busy with their own con-cerns. But the Ribono shel Olam understood. Not a second could be lost. At the very moment that Yosef was sold into Egypt, the Ribono shel Olam began to busy Himself with the creation of the "light" of Moshiach.

Clearly, Rashi had his reasons for choosing as he did and we certainly have no right to attempt to correct him. However, for our purposes let us use this midrash as an alternative sug-gestion to explain the insertion. It is my contention that, if we accept this, it can help us to understand significant differ-ences between the final verse in the Yosef saga that *precedes* the Yehudah/Tamar segment and the first verse in the Yosef saga that *follows* the Yehudah/Tamar segment. We noted above that the latter verse, for reasons of its own, gives us in-formation we already know from earlier on. However, it does so by means of highly significant adjustments to the wording.

Let us look at these two verses next to one another.

BEREISHIS 37:28 AND 37:36	BEREISHIS 39:1
כח. ויביאו את יוסף מצרימה	א. ויוסף הורד מצרים
לו. והמדנים מכרו אתו אל מצרים לפוטיפר סריס פרעה שר הטבחים	ויקנהו פוטיפר סריס פרעה שר הטבחים איש מצרי
28. They brought Yosef to Egypt	1. Now Yosef was taken down to Egypt
36. The Medanim sold him in Egypt to Potiphar, Pharaoh's minister, the chief butcher.	And Potiphar, Pharaoh's minister, the chief butcher, an Egyptian citizen, bought him.

In the earlier passage the merchants are the subject; Yosef is no more than the object of their actions. *They* brought him [not "took him *down*," an expression denoting exile] to Egypt, and sold him there to one Potiphar, who happened to be a minister and chief butcher to the royal household. This Potiphar has no particular significance, and there is no need to apprise us of his citizenship. For our purposes, it is all one whether he was a foreigner who happened to be living in Egypt, or whether he was an Egyptian.

In Bereishis, chapter 39, the merchants are of no interest at all; Yosef, the hapless slave dragged down to Egypt against his will, is at the center of the drama. Potiphar [as a significant actor, not simply a prop to whom the merchants happened to sell their booty] buys him. An issue is made of the fact that he is an Egyptian. The Torah knows that Egypt has been designated as the land in which the Bris bein HaBesarim would be fulfilled[6] and considers it significant that Yosef's exile was at the hands of a son of that people.

What has happened? Why does Bereishis 39:1 present information we already know, in such a radically different manner? The answer of course lies in the saga of Yehudah and Tamar, which has since become a part of the record. The knowledge that, behind the scenes of the Yosef drama, the Ribono shel Olam had begun to busy Himself with creating the "light" of the Moshiach, has shifted the weight of what until now had been an ordinary business transaction, into a national watershed. History was on the march and nothing along the route could be "ordinary" anymore.

In the eyes of the midrash we have now adopted, Yehudah and Tamar, people ostensibly involved in a complex of family relationships, appear to have been little more than stick figures moved around by the Ribono shel Olam as actors in a drama that was vastly larger and grander than their personal concerns. That much is made clear in the Chazal we plan to examine in the next chapter. But Chazal do not make clear, and for us it is of vital importance to understand, why that drama required such a strange plot. Why does the creation of the "light" of the Moshiach require that the great Tamar must debase herself and sit by the wayside disguised as a common prostitute? Why does holy Yehudah have to find himself in the embarrassing situation of being drawn helplessly toward a disgraceful union that must have cost him dreadful shame? Why initiate the sacred edifice of Messianic fulfillment by such ugly means?

Above all, what exactly is the "light" of Moshiach? Why not simply "Moshiach"?

These are issues we will have to confront in the next chapter. Come, we have much to learn.

EIGHTEEN

Yehudah And Tamar II

e have one non-negotiable point of departure. Great events, certainly great events which are recorded in TaNaCh, don't just happen. They come about as the Ribono shel Olam determines that they are to come about. It is up to us to learn seriously and think deeply. Beyond that lies understanding or silence. There are no alternatives.

So why Yehudah and Tamar? Why Boaz and Rus? Why, for that matter Lot and his two daughters through whom he became the progenitor of Moav, the dreadful cradle within which Rus, mother of Dovid and ultimately the Melech HaMoshiach, was nurtured?[1]

I have an idea which I would like to share with you.

First, it is necessary to set the record straight about the story. We recall that after the brothers had sold Yosef on Yehudah's advice, Yehudah "went down" from his brothers and married a woman of whom we know very little.[2] Rashi records the Chazal that Yehudah "went down" in the sense that his brothers demoted him from his royal position, because they felt that he had let them down. They claimed that, had he asserted his moral standing to demand that Yosef be returned to his father, they would have listened.

We may assume that, after such recriminations, Yehudah's frame of mind was not a happy one. If what the brothers said was true, then he had failed miserably in his role of "king". The first responsibility of leadership is to recognize the potential of his people and to prod them and guide them towards growth and self-fulfillment. By underestimating them he had blundered inexcusably.

Tragedy continued to plague him. Of three sons that were born to him, two died in short order. Both, one after the other, had married Tamar and died almost immediately afterwards. Bereaved and broken, Yehudah now had to consider his duties towards his twice widowed daughter-in-law. She seemed to expect that she would be given in marriage to the youngest son, Sheilah. Yehudah, understandably fearing for Sheilah's life had no intention of permitting this union. Nevertheless he made a vague promise that once Sheilah grew up, Tamar could expect to be married to him.

It did not take long for Tamar to realize that that promise would not be kept. Nevertheless she was determined to remain within Yehudah's family and chose the only path open to her. She disguised herself as a harlot and sat by the wayside waiting for Yehudah to pass by. Her ploy was successful and Yehudah did indeed consort with her, unaware that she was Tamar. From that union twins were born, one of whom—Peretz—was to become the progenitor of the Dovidic family.

How are we to understand Yehudah? On the surface it would seem that we have already offered a sufficiently convincing answer in the past few paragraphs. He was a broken man. He was disgusted with himself for failing so tragically with his brothers, convinced that the Ribono shel Olam had cast him aside; else why would he have lost his two sons so precipitously? As if all that was not enough, he must have been acutely aware of having misused the guiltless and defenseless widow. He had lied to her and misled her with false hopes which doomed her to the pain of shattered dreams.

There was precious little that he could respect in himself at this point in his life. Perhaps it is not difficult to understand how, in such a state of mind, he had sought the comfort of forgetfulness with the harlot by the wayside.[3]

I think I have made a creditable case which might well be true. The fact is that it is utterly wrong and indeed, on my part, utterly wrongheaded to have even suggested it. Let us see how Chazal described what happened. They also knew all that I have suggested and yet rejected it completely. Why were they right and I so hopelessly wrong? The answer can only be that they knew who the Avos were, knew who the Shevatim were. They knew that these great spiritual heroes cannot be cut down to size, to fit into the silly little banalities which make up our lives.

Enough said. Let us turn to the midrash and learn what really happened.

אמר ר' יוחנן בקש לעבור וזימן לו הקב"ה מלאך שהוא ממונה על התאוה
אמר לו יהודה היכן אתה הולך מהיכן מלכים עומדים מהיכן גדולים עומדים
ויט אליה אל הדרך בע"כ שלא בטובתו.

R. Yochanan taught, Yehudah wanted to pass by [the
harlot who was sitting by the wayside]. Immediately
God summoned the angel whose charge it is to generate
desire. This angel said, "Yehudah! Where are you going?
[Consider, if you will not allow yourself to be bewitched
by this woman] from where will kings arise? From where
will great leaders come? [Upon hearing this] Yehudah
turned towards her by the wayside. It was against his
will, against his better judgment.

The difference between the midrash's perception of what
happened and the description which I presented earlier is
clear enough and there is no need to go over it once more.
However, having now read the midrash we are struck by the
question which we asked earlier but which has now become
immeasurably more forceful. What did the angel mean when
he argued that Yehudah simply must succumb to his desires,
else from where would kings and leaders stem? Was this then
the only way? It seems very clear that we are not being told
that *even though* this does not seem a straight and holy path,
nevertheless it can lead to the sanctity of messianic kingship. It
is not *even though* but *because*! The crooked path of Yehudah's
union with Tamar was not a possible way but the only way in
which the kingship could come about. How are we to understand this?

In the previous chapter we saw the midrash which tells us
that while all the other interested parties were taking care of
their own needs, the Ribono shel Olam was busy laying the
groundwork for the "light" of the Moshiach. The time has
come to ask ourselves what this "light" might be. What is the
difference between saying that the Ribono shel Olam was preparing the way for Moshiach or saying that He was preparing
the way for the "light" of the Moshiach?[4]

It was Chol HaMo'ed Succos when I was thinking about
these matters, and it suddenly struck me that the answer to

my question had been staring me in my face since the haftora of the first day of Yom Tov.

Here is what the prophet Zechariah (chapter 14 verse 7) has to say about the time when Moshiach will finally come to us:

והיה יום אחד הוא יודע ליהוה לא יום ולא לילה והיה לעת ערב יהיה אור.

There shall be a day, known [only] to God, which will be neither day nor night. And it shall come about when evening falls that there will be a light.

Here is Metzudos to this verse:

והיה יום אחד זה יתמיד יום אחד ונודע הוא לה' מתי יהיה היום הזה אשר לא יהיה לא יום ולא לילה כי לא ידעו מה הוא הטובה אם רעה. **לעת ערב** סמוך לערב יהיה אור ר"ל אז יכירו בטובת התשועה.

All the forgoing will take place within the span of one day, a day known only to God which will be neither day nor night. This is the description of a time of confusion when it will be impossible to be sure whether what is happening is good or bad. However, when evening falls, when darkness begins to envelope all, there will be light. Then salvation will become apparent to all

I will resist the temptation to attempt to identify the period[5] during which confusion is expected to reign. I suspect that in every single generation during our dreadful *galus* experience, people would have recognized their own times as fitting that description.[6] I would like to focus upon a different question. Why will the light of understanding become apparent to all specifically as evening[7] falls? Why should the bright light of understanding choose particularly a moment of lowering darkness to break out?

The answer seems clear to me. To the extent that we have any perception at all about what the Messianic redemption might portend, it is that it will be a time of knowledge, an understanding and clarification of all that had been hidden until then. Rambam (Melachim 12:5) ends his description of the *Yemos HaMoshiach* with the words, *For the land will be filled with knowledge of HaShem even as the sea water covers the ocean bed* (Yeshayahu 11:9). I believe that this particular *pasuk* brings us a very special message. We know that the sea bed is an extremely variegated landscape. There are towering mountains and deep, deep valleys and gorges. The ocean of knowledge will cover them—read "equalize" them—all. The ups and downs of history, the times of Israel's rejoicing and mourning, all, all will be equal in our eyes. Every movement and moment will be understood and treasured.

The Messianic epoch is the time when darkness will turn into light, distance into proximity, confusion into clarity and questions will turn into answers.

I want to suggest that we have discovered the explanation for why the cradle of the monarchy was rocked by such ambiguous winds. The cradle of the monarchy is the cradle of the Melech HaMoshiach whose function it will be to eliminate all ambiguities. The time will come when we will understand it all. That is what Moshiach is all about.

This, I believe, is the answer to the question which caused us so much anguish at the end of the previous chapter. We were unable to understand why Yehudah and Tamar *had* to come together in so ugly a manner, why Boaz *had* to find Rus lying at his feet in the middle of the night and why, at the very dawn of the history of the monarchy, the Moabite nation *had* to be produced through Lot's incestuous relationship with his daughter.

I believe that now we have an answer. The moments and events in which the monarchy was conceived were the moments and events in which the Messianic era, at least in potential, made its entry into history. As we have defined this era, it is the time when the light of absolute understanding will illuminate even the darkest corners of our experiences, the time when all that had appeared as evil, twisted and ugly will be revealed as having been a part of the Ribono shel Olam's plan. As Pesachim 50a puts it, it will be the time when even over what appears to us as tragedy, we will make the blessing, *HaTov VeHaMeitiv,* Who *is* good and Who by His very nature, will do *only* good.

The pivotal couplings in the establishment of the messianic line: Lot and his daughters; Yehudah and his Tamar; Boaz and his Rus, all were fraught with ambiguities because these were meant to teach us that it is the nature of Moshiach not to be daunted by appearances. When directed by the Ribono shel Olam, means can be sanctified by ends, and surface question marks can find their answers in the depths of divine wisdom and understanding.

All this will have repercussions for our understanding of the Dovid/Bas Sheva saga. To round things off we will require a new chapter. Come! We have much to do.

NINETEEN

Dovid's Mistake

*I*t is difficult to climb down from the "high" I experienced in the previous chapter when I discovered—or think and hope I discovered—the meaning of the "light" of Moshiach. After that—always assuming that I was right—everything is a little bit of a letdown. Still, we have work to do. Specifically, given all that we now understand, we must ask ourselves why Dovid was wrong in his assessment of what the sudden appearance of Bas Sheva was meant to portend. Was he not justified in viewing himself as part of the straight line: Yehudah/Tamar—Boaz/Rus—Dovid/Bas Sheva? How was he supposed to know that this grape that was so obviously his for the grasping was as yet unripe?[1]

Let us look back at what exactly happened after that arrow's fateful journey, and determine which of Dovid's actions might have been judged sinful by the Ribono shel Olam. Dovid sent for Bas Sheva. When she came to him, he consorted with her. Subsequently he brings Uriah back from the front and orders him to go home to his wife. He assumes that then Uriah will consort with Bas Sheva and that any child that would be born from Dovid's association with her would be assumed by everybody to be Uriah's child. But Uriah refuses to go home. Uriah feels that if he were to seek out the comfort of his own bed, it would be a betrayal of his comrades who were out in the field, subject to the discomforts and dangers of the battlefront. Dovid sends Uriah back to rejoin the army while ordering his general, Yoav, to position Uriah in the most dangerously exposed position so that he would certainly be killed.

Nathan the prophet comes to Dovid and spins a story custom-made to arouse the king's fury: the wealthy bully who steals his poor neighbor's single sheep offends against many of those virtues that Dovid holds dear throughout his meditations in Tehilim. Justice, compassion, a craving for sanctity with its concomitant rejection of self-indulgence, all these and many others are trampled underfoot by the overweening callousness, crassness, and insensitivity of the story's villain. Nathan asks Dovid what punishment ought to be meted out to this brute. Horrified at the sheer mean-spiritedness of the perpetrator, Dovid responds that nothing but the death penalty will do. Nathan tells Dovid, "You are that man!" Dovid, understanding the metaphor and realizing the justice of the accusation, immediately admits his guilt.

We started off by asking which of Dovid's actions the Ribono shel Olam might have considered sinful. A superficial reading of what we have offered here would surely place the fact that Bas Sheva was married to Uriah at the top of the list. Dovid apparently had relations with a woman who was wife to another. Beyond that there is the conspiracy to have Uriah killed. That, too, seems to qualify as a truly heinous crime.

A simple reading of the story, however, shows that these two cannot possibly have been the transgressions for which Nathan came to excoriate Dovid. Had either of them been on Nathan's mind, he would not have had to resort to stories about sheep and abusive neighbors. Sins such as those need no parables to highlight their horror. Nathan's approach makes it abundantly clear that he had other matters on his mind.

Why not these two? For this we have the tradition of Chazal (Shabbos 56a) that, in fact, Dovid never transgressed either of them.[2] Uriah had given his wife a *get* before he went out to battle, as did all the soldiers in Dovid's army. It was considered prudent in order to avoid any *agunah* problems that might arise if they were to be killed with no witnesses to testify to their death. It transpires that, in fact, Bas Sheva was not bound to Uriah at the time.[3] Moreover, Dovid was justified in arranging Uriah's death. Uriah had incurred the death penalty. He had spoken to Dovid with less than the requisite respect, thus placing himself in the category of a *mored bemalchus,* one who rebels against the king.

How, then, had Dovid erred? The answer to that question lies at the core of Nathan's parable. Dovid had not been sensitive to the hurt that he was causing Uriah, who, at the time when the fateful arrow flew, had not yet been guilty of anything. It is true that Uriah, in accordance with common usage, had given Bas Sheva a *get*, but he and she had every expectation of reuniting once he came back unharmed from the Ammonite campaign. Dovid, who had so much of his own, had been willing to perpetrate violence against a defenseless subject and take his all. For that, Nathan implied and Dovid confirmed, there could be no forgiveness.

Before we gleaned this insight, we had built our defense of Dovid by arguing that he could reasonably have supposed this strange confluence of circumstances to be the challenge with which the Ribono shel Olam had promised to test his mettle. He would, as his ancestors Yehudah and Boaz had done before him, rise to the occasion and do what he was called upon to do. What in lesser people would have been a capitulation to carnal desire would for him be an act of service to the Ribono shel Olam performed in sanctity and purity.

But he was wrong. He had misjudged the Ribono shel Olam badly. There was one vital difference among Yehudah/Tamar, Boaz/Rus, and himself. In those earlier cases no innocents were hurt. Here there was Uriah, eagerly and legitimately anticipating a reunion with his former wife. Dovid should have realized that the Ribono shel Olam would not build Malchus Beis Dovid on the back of a human tragedy.[4]

TWENTY

Tying up Some Loose Ends

We are nearing the end of the book and must now shoulder the daunting task of summing up what we have learned in nineteen difficult chapters. As we gather up the various threads that we have developed in those chapters so that we can weave a coherent picture that we would then be able to analyze, it would be advisable if you, dear reader, took the time to reread some of the salient parts. There is a lot going on in this book and a single reading may not be enough to internalize the implications.

In particular I would suggest that at this point you reread chapters 9, 10, and 11. Those three essays really contain the chief elements of the conclusions toward which our analysis in this last chapter will point.

The lion's share of chapter 9 is taken up by the profound analysis of Sefer Tehilim offered by Dr. Henry Bieberfeld in his *David, King of Israel*. Let us together read a few paragraphs from that larger piece:

> David's mind, responsive as no other, found in the omnipresence of God the one experience that became the dominant force in his life, the atmosphere and living-space of his existence.
>
> When the supreme "event" of the idea of God was perceived by David, an experience was born of such singular force that it reverberates through the ages. The psalms are the record of that great union, when the impact of the omnipresence of God struck the responsive chords of David's being....
>
> Thus nature, the profusion of phenomena filling the world, made the chords of David's soul sing. One unending melody reverberates from it—God. This universal theme resounds from all directions of the cosmos. Space is filled with it, for "the heavens declare the glory of God" and "the earth is the Lord's." Time proclaims it, for: "Day unto day uttereth speech and night unto night showeth

knowledge." Nature is but one aspect of the divine, null and void without the life-giving presence of His might.

There we have as clear a definition of Sefer Tehilim as we are likely to find anywhere. The problem is that it does not seem to cohere with the picture of Dovid that is conveyed to us in Sefer Shmuel.

In Sefer Shmuel we meet Dovid as a very fallible king, prone to make mistakes that had dreadful repercussions for his people. Let us recall the midrash from Devarim Rabba 5:11, which we quoted in chapter 3.

> God said to us, "In these pre-Messianic times you asked that I grant you kings to rule over you. I complied with your request and gave you kings. You soon found out that these caused you untold troubles. There was Shaul whose war cost many lives on Mount Gilbo'a. *Dovid brought a plague upon you* and Achav, a drought. Tzidkiyahu caused the Beis HaMikdash to be destroyed."

Here, Chazal themselves put the Dovid of Shmuel in very unflattering company, listing him together with Achav and Tzidkiyahu as proof that the monarchy occasionally proved to be a major tragedy for the people.

Indeed, as you may recall from chapters 5, 6, and 7, we elected to follow Malbim in his idea that Dovid had certain leanings toward a self-assertion that could easily lead to sin. In Malbim's eyes this propensity had been a positive factor in the context of the monarchy. Dovid would know how to strike a balance between the warring parts of his personality and would use each trait in only those situations to which it was appropriate. That may be true but, by its very nature, such a conflicted personality cannot always come down on the right side. We learned from R. Tzadok (Tzidkas HaTzadik, section 244; see chapter 6) that this very turbulence in Dovid's nature, the fact that there really were *warring* elements in his character, disqualified Dovid from building the Beis HaMikdash. It created instability where stability was the sine qua non for inviting the Shechinah to dwell among us.

The series of errors involved in the Dovid/Bas Sheva saga, which we examined in detail in chapters 12–19, are not the only examples. We also have the devastating judgment of Shabbos 56b that the tragic split in the kingdom between Rechav'om and Yerov'om was foreordained in the moment when Dovid accepted *lashon hara* about Yehonoson's son Mipiboshes and ruled that the disputed field was to be split between him and Tziva (II Shmuel 19:30).[1]

In chapter 11 we mooted the possibility that the Godly spirit that entered Dovid at his investiture inspired him only sporadically and that it seemed possible that those actions of Dovid criticized either in TaNaCh itself or by Chazal took place when the spirit was not upon him.

If that suggestion has any truth to it, the teshuvah that followed immediately upon Nathan's reproach after the Bas Sheva incident becomes perhaps the most significant event in the trek of the historic Dovid to the Messianic Dovid. We will devote the next chapter, the one that brings this small study to its conclusion, to this topic. In the meantime I would recommend the conscientious reader to look back to chapter 8 (particularly note 11), chapter 10 (particularly note 14), and chapter 19 (particularly note 2). These are locations at which I already anticipated what the end of the book would be.

Come, join me in studying this last exciting chapter.

TWENTY-ONE

Dovid Is Alive and Will Endure

he time has come to bring this little book to a close. We have thought a lot and learned a lot but I have the feeling that all of us, you dear reader as well as I, still feel a measure of discomfort at the picture of Dovid HaMelech we have gleaned from Sefer Shmuel. The failings that we have traced seem too pervasive to fit our perception of the precursor of the Melech HaMoshiach.

We must make a final effort to understand Dovid Ha-Melech a little better.

We can do this best by listening once more to what Dovid thought of himself as he was nearing the end of his life.

Let us return to our discussion of the difficult, almost truncated psalm that turned out to be the very last composition of Israel's sweet singer. In chapter 11 we wondered whether, as he began to put his thoughts together, Dovid already intuited that the Godly spirit from which he had always drawn his inspiration was beginning to ebb from him. We thought that if, indeed, he had such fears, this would explain the long and complex description of himself in the opening verse. He was, so we thought, lining up those qualities that he knew defined his spiritual personality so that they might stand by him and he might draw upon them this one last time.

Here is the list: *Dovid son of Yishai; the man who was* HUKAM OL; *he who was anointed by Yaakov's God; the one who imbued Israel's songs with delight.*

If we were right in this assumption, then in this list we have an intimate self-portrayal of the elusive Dovid whom we are trying to find.

So who was Dovid?

We will analyze each of these four categories separately so that we may the better understand the composite picture, which is of course what we are after.

1. *Dovid son of Yishai*: Shabbos 55b and Bava Basra 17a teach that, of all mankind, only four died as a result of the "wiles of

the snake." These were people who lived lives of total innocence and would have lived eternally were it not for the fact
that Adam had sinned. They were: Yaakov's son, Binyomin;
Moshe Rabbeinu's father, Amrom; Dovid's father, Yishai; and
Dovid's son, Kil'ov.

Maharal (Chidushei Aggada) discusses these ideas in both
places. The passage that I wish to use is the one in Shabbos.
I do not pretend to understand what Maharal says in any
depth, but he does touch upon a question that, I believe, any
of us would ask. How are we to understand that both Dovid's
father and Dovid's son attained the exalted level of having
lived absolutely pure lives, while Dovid himself fell short?[1]

Maharal's answer reads approximately as follows: Dovid's
failings were the result of the fact that his *madreigah* was so
exalted that it was impossible for any human as a human to
live up to it constantly. He sinned, not because he was a "sin-
ner," but because failings were built into the very fabric of his
being.

Here, then, is the first of the four insights that will, in aggregate, give us the full portrait we are seeking. By imbuing
Dovid with a potential greatness that lifted him to a level that
in real terms would be impossible to sustain, God guaranteed that Dovid's life would not be totally blameless.[2] From
the moment of his anointment,[3] it was guaranteed that Dovid
would live a turbulent life of struggle, punctuated by occasional lapses.

2. *HaGever Hukam Ol:* In chapter 11 we translated this
phrase as, *he who has been raised on high.* Here is why. *Hukam*
is the *hoph'al* (the passive form of *kum* in the causative case
[*hiph'il*], to raise up). The active form would be *heikim.* Thus,
in our context, *who was raised. Ol* can mean *upward* (compare
Hoshe'a 11:7). So, *who has been raised on high.*

However, Mo'ed Katan 16b reads the phrase as though it
meant, *who established the yoke of repentance.*[4] This challenges
us to answer a number of questions. What exactly is "the yoke
of teshuvah"? What is meant by saying that Dovid "established" it? Third, and in my opinion particularly irksome, why

express a thought that involves the active form *heikim* with the passive, *hukam*?

So what is the "the yoke of teshuvah"? The late, great Rav Hutner (Yom HaKipurim 6:10) explains that it describes the inevitability of ultimate teshuvah. We have been promised that our world, when history will have run its course, will end up right. There is no chance that "free will" will, in a ghastly ending, topple God's purpose in creation. Free will is indeed absolute, but it is not absolutely absolute. There is one tiny, but oh so significant, brake on its freedom. It cannot, ultimately, frustrate God's purpose. A yoke implies guaranteed results, the power to enforce, to limit or eliminate options. We will, we absolutely will, do teshuvah in the end. That is "the yoke of teshuvah."

In what sense did Dovid "establish" it? If you look back to chapter 10, note 9, you will come across the midrash that teaches that Dovid's seventy years of life were a gift to him from Adam. God had told Adam that a "Dovid" was to be born, but that no years of life had been allotted to him. Adam donated seventy of the thousand years that had been set aside as his portion. I have been taught that the meaning of this strange tradition is as follows. Dovid's purpose in life was to "establish the yoke of teshuvah." Had Adam not sinned, no teshuvah would ever have been required. Adam "donated" the years that Dovid was destined to live, in the sense that he gave purpose to Dovid's life.

Dovid's task in life was to make teshuvah an integral part of Jewish existence. He would define it and create it in its fullness. He established the "yoke," the inevitability of teshuvah.

So how does *heikim* (active) in the *d'rash* become *hukam* (passive) in the text? I firmly believe that what we learned in the last few paragraphs provides us with an answer that looks and feels so simple that the very ease with which it suggests itself seems to me to attest to its truth.

It is true that Dovid "established" (active) the yoke of teshuvah. It is equally true that what he did was foreordained. He was, so to speak, made to do it (passive). The mathematics works simply enough: a.) Dovid was gifted with an inner spiritual standing, which made it inevitable that, along the way, there would be failures that would require repentance (Maharal, above). b.) The very sweep of time that constituted his life span was, so to speak, on loan to him from Adam, only because he would use that gift to establish teshuvah in all its properties, including its ultimate inevitability. There was much in Dovid's life that simply had to occur. The *"heikim"* was very much a *"hukam."*

3. *He who was anointed by Yaakov's God:* Why of all the *avos* mention Yaakov? Why, in fact, mention anybody at all? Why not just *Moshiach HaShem* as Dovid himself constantly referred to Shaul (see I Shmuel 24:6 and onward)?

I recall that I once heard the relationship of the *avos* to Eretz Yisrael described as follows: Avraham—the first one who came; Yitzchak—the first one who remained; Yaakov—the first one who returned. Yaakov is the one among the patriarchs who taught that exile need not destroy.[5] He came back whole from his exile in Lavan's home. Actually, I believe that this is expressed in Midrash Tanchuma, Naso, on Tehilim 77:14: The Ribono shel Olam said to Yosef,[6] "Yosef, the merits that you and Yaakov have accrued will be responsible for Israel's redemption." That is the meaning of the verse in Tehilim, *You have redeemed your people, the children of Yaakov and Yosef, with the full force of your might.*

Dovid, who knows that it is from his descendants that Moshiach will arise, feels that his anointment as the progenitor of the ultimate redeemer came to him from "Yaakov's God."

4. *The one who imbued Israel's songs with the power to delight:* In this final chapter, I would like to share with you, dear reader, an idea that struck me about the nature of Sefer Tehilim in contrast to Sefer Shmuel. It would be a good idea if, at this point, you would take the time to glance back at chapters 9 and 10, paying particular attention to the excerpt from Henry Bieberfeld's *David, King of Israel,* where we began to think about this issue. Here we will strike out in a new direction.

My sense of what might define Sefer Tehilim would provide, if it is at all correct, an adequate answer to the nagging problem we raised there, why Sefer Shmuel ignores Dovid's Tehilim activities almost completely. We wondered why at least those *mizmorim* that are identified as having been composed under the impression of various events described in Shmuel should not have been recorded there. It does seem that it would have made sense to complete the picture of Dovid's state of mind at that time.

The verb, *N'im*, "to imbue with delight," packs a great deal of power. It is a daring phrase. Normally we would say that one man's delight might well be another man's boredom. Tastes differ and a thought, a phrase, a tune that touches one person to his very core may leave another cold. Henry Bieberfeld's description of Sefer Tehilim, which we quoted in chapter 9, did, I think, hit exactly the right tone. He speaks of Tehilim as incorporating triumphs and tragedies, periods of calm and unrest, of supreme confidence and hopeless despair, mystic surrender and moral reflections, universal love and implacable wrath. Does it stand to reason that all these themes would delight all of us?

So where are we to go from here? It seems to me that we have only one sensible route and that is to question what "delight" in this context really means. In what sense are Israel's songs, particularly those that are recorded in Sefer Tehilim, delightful?

I think the passage from Dr. Bieberfeld that we quoted in chapter 11 points us in the correct direction. Here is another quote from there.

> David's real life is recorded in the psalms. This is the true mirror of his being, reflecting every phase of his life. *If the historical books show the outward contours of his image, the psalms probe the deepest secrets. The psalms are his world, the world of the idea of God with all its variety. It is a world detached from and beyond the material sphere. Hence allusions to actual events occur only rarely in psalms. The historical books provide the form to be filled in with idea and experience* [italics mine].

I have italicized the last few sentences because that is the part I really want to consider now. The earlier part of the paragraph is there only in order to lend context.

What is Bieberfeld saying?[7] He is saying that Sefer Tehilim is infused with the "idea of God." What are these sentences *really* saying? I believe that they are laying out for us the secret of the relationship between Sefer Tehilim and Sefer Shmuel. They are saying that Sefer Shmuel is a this-worldly book and Sefer Tehilim is a Messianic book. They are telling us that these books are as they are, that they do as they do, act as they act, and experience as they experience, because they inhabit radically different worlds. It says that the two books are so different because Dovid Melech Yisrael, the Melech HaMoshiach, lived a complex life that found expression at two levels. When the divine spirit was upon him his world was suffused with holiness, there were no barriers between him and the Ribono shel Olam, and from that standpoint he knew and felt that every moment of his life, the triumphs and tragedies, the periods of calm and unrest, those of supreme confidence and hopeless despair, periods when he was given to mystic surrender or moral reflections, universal love or implacable wrath, all of those and myriad others indefinable and beyond communication, all, were gifted directly by the Ribono shel Olam Whose presence he felt constantly. Tehilim were, so to speak, written in paradise.

The events recorded in Sefer Shmuel were different. They belonged, literally and experientially, in the here and now, with all the ambiguities and uncertainties, the victories and the defeats, the moments of high connection and those of bottomless despair. They were as true in the context in which they took place as were the descriptions in Sefer Tehilim within their very special universe. Sefer Shmuel does not record the Tehilim, even those that were composed in the context of the events it records, because they did not belong in its world.

We asked why all Tehilim without exception are meant to delight. The answer, I believe, is because the unmediated presence and experience of the Ribono shel Olam is a delight. It was, after all, Dovid who sang, *Kindness and sternness will stimulate me to jubilation* (Tehilim 101:1).[8] To which Chazal comment, "I will jubilate as sincerely when You are stern with me as when You are kind (Berachos 60b).[9]

Let us now return to the portrait of the elusive Dovid that, so we promised ourselves, we would find after a conscientious examination of the four titles with which Dovid apparently felt urged to introduce his final composition.

They are: that he was prone to sin; that the purpose of his life was to introduce the inevitability of teshuvah into the very fabric of his people; that his Messianic future entailed the redemption of Israel from exile; and that the Tehilim which he composed introduce a taste of the Messianic future into Jewish history, as it was and is being lived in the pre-Messianic era.

We were concerned with the many failings that, at a superficial reading, seem somehow to have dimmed the luster of Dovid Melech Yisrael as he is portrayed in Sefer Shmuel. We now understand that these were all a part of his Messianic destiny, which was and is the defining feature of his very identity. The coming of Moshiach is inextricably bound up with teshuvah.[10] The stories we are offered in Sefer Shmuel are the stories of the *"gever hukam ol."*

We began this book with a contemplation of Israel's affinity with the moon and the cryptic phrase, "Dovid, King of Israel, lives and endures," which is a significant component of our monthly Kidush HaChodesh. We will end up with the same theme. Our research is going to lengthen this chapter considerably, but in the end we will be happy that we took the time. The section will be a good and satisfying rounding off of our contemplation of Dovid Melech Yisrael.

Here is a *tefilah* that is a part of our monthly Kidush Levanah.

Let it be Your will, HaShem, my God and the God of my fathers, to fill in the missing component of the moon so that there be no diminution of it at all. Then the light of the moon will be as [bright as] the light of the sun as it was before it was made smaller. As it is written, *the two great luminaries.*

Moreover, may the verse which is written (Hoshe'a 3:5),...*then they will seek out HaShem their God and Dovid their king,* be fulfilled for us. Amen.[11]

If some of you are like I am, you will probably have said this passage for many years and never given it very careful thought. That would be a pity for you as it is for me. In an attempted rectification, I would like to discuss two aspects of the passage. The first is to clarify to myself why I should care whether or not the moon appears to me to be complete or not. I know that the moon has no light of its own and that it is only its and the earth's movements that determine how much of it will be visible to people on earth. I am not in the least concerned by the fact that my view of the moon gets diminished as it moves along its orbit. On the contrary, I enjoy observing the waxing and the waning that happen so predictably every month. So, for what exactly am I praying? And, why should I care whether the moon is smaller than the sun or the same size? It all sounds very mysterious to me.

Then there is the matter of the second paragraph. Is it related to the first one or not? The *vav* with which it starts clearly ties the two together. Why? In what sense are the two related? More specifically, what is Dovid HaMelech's place in this context? Why should our longing to be reunited with him be connected with the size and completeness of the moon?

Let us begin our search with Rashi to Rosh Hashanah 25a. There Rashi points out that Dovid's kingship is compared to the moon, but he does not explain why and in what sense this is so.[12]

There must be many deep insights hidden in this comparison,[13] but at a simple level it seems to me that when we recall Dovid's identity as the *hukam ol,* the one who established the yoke of teshuvah, it is not really difficult to see a strong connection. The minute we look upon the sinful state as one of distance from the Ribono shel Olam, teshuvah falls read-

ily enough into a moonlike edging forward, an elimination of
barriers, a return to a loving embrace.

Let us listen to Rambam (Hilchos Teshuvah 7:7):

כמה מעולה מעלת התשובה אמש היה זה מובדל מה' אלהי ישראל שנאמר
עונותיכם היו מבדילים ביניכם לבין אלהיכם צועק ואינו נענה שנאמר כי
תרבו תפלה וגו' ועושה מצות וטורפין אותן בפניו שנאמר מי בקש זאת
מידכם רמוס חצרי מי גם בכם ויסגר דלתים וגו' והיום הוא מודבק בשכינה
שנאמר ואתם הדבקים בה' אלהיכם צועק ונענה מיד שנאמר והיה טרם
יקראו ואני אענה ועושה מצות ומקבלין אותן בנחת ושמחה שנאמר כי
כבר רצה האלהים את מעשיך ולא עוד אלא שמתאוים להם שנאמר וערבה
לה' מנחת יהודה וירושלם כימי עולם וכשנים קדמוניות.

How great are the benefits of teshuvah! Yesterday this
person was *separated from the Ribono shel Olam,* as it is
written, *Your sins have become a barrier between you and
your God: He cried out but was not answered...did worthy deeds but these were rejected to his face...but today he
cleaves to the Shechinah....He cries out and the response
is immediate...does worthy deeds and these are happily accepted,* and more, the Ribono shel Olam actually
craves them.

The imagery is striking, is it not? We have a movement from
a state of being locked away from the Ribono shel Olam by
the barrier of sin, to one in which the barrier is removed and
there is a renewed closeness to God.

The step between this picture and the waxing and waning
moon is small indeed. Why, after all, is half the moon always
dark, if not because that half faces away from the sun, thus
preventing the sun's rays from quickening its frigid surface
with its embrace of warmth and light? [14]

I have the feeling that we are getting close to some significant truths. For example, we begin to have an inkling of why
the "missing component" of the moon should cause us anguish
and why we should pray that the Ribono shel Olam eliminate this gap once and for all. Without worrying too much
about the technicalities, something that we can leave to the
Ribono shel Olam, we can still understand that this chunk of

darkness speaks to us of alienation. Absence speaks to us of presence. When we look up at the void, we know that we are really looking at a mighty sphere but cannot see it. Its obstinate insistence on maintaining its orientation away from the sun denies it the light of reconciliation. We do not want to be brought face-to-face with such self-destructive cantankerousness. What we want is to be good, very good, and always good. We want the time to come when the constant cycle of repulsion and attraction comes to an end. We want to do teshuvah, a full and lasting teshuvah, so that not even a sliver of our being is ever blocked again from the Ribono shel Olam's smile.

Neither my astronomy nor my knowledge of how to read a *pasuk* in Chumash is particularly informed, but I suspect that when the Ribono shel Olam "made the moon small," he changed it from being a star, like the sun, into being a satellite "attached" to earth by gravity. When we pray that the moon might one day become "large" again, what we are really asking is that the kingship of Dovid be cut loose from its "attachment" to the earth.[15] It will have earned its status as an independent "star" generating its own light.

We have just now described the *yoke of teshuvah* that it was Dovid's task to establish. Now let us return to the issue of the second paragraph and see what sense we can make of it. Here it is again:

> Moreover, may the verse which is written (Hoshe'a 3:5) *...then they will seek out HaShem their God and Dovid their king,* be fulfilled for us. Amen.

As we noted above, this prayer seems to grow out of the earlier ones. We are now ready to see how this is so. Let us first sum up what it is for which we are asking. It is this. We are asking for the actualization of the promise contained in the verse that says that once the Ribono shel Olam will have replaced the missing component of the moon, once the two heavenly bodies will once more be of equal size, then it can be anticipated that we will once more seek out *HaShem [our] God and Dovid our king.*

What is the connection to that which went before?

Here I think that I can suggest a solid answer that, I believe, will bear out the thesis I have developed in explaining the two requests about the moon in terms of a general teshuvah.

I do this by the simple means of learning the *pasuk* we quote in its context in Hoshe'a. Here is the *pasuk* as quoted in our *tefilah*:

ובקשו את יהוה אלהיהם ואת דויד מלכם.

And they will seek out HaShem their God and Dovid their king.

Here is the full *pasuk* from Hoshe'a 3:5:

אחר ישבו בני ישראל ובקשו את יהוה אלהיהם ואת דוד מלכם ופחדו אל יהוה ואל טובו באחרית הימים.

After that, the Children of Israel *will repent* and seek out HaShem their God and Dovid their king and live in awe of HaShem and His goodness, at the end of days.

Is it not interesting that the very verse that seems to grow out of our prayers concerning the moon mentions that this seeking out of both HaShem and Dovid HaMelech will come about as a result of just one thing and that is teshuvah? Does this not seem to confirm all that we have said concerning the relationship between the moon's peregrinations away from and toward the sun and the concept of repentance?

I hope that you will agree that we now understand Dovid HaMelech a little better than we did before we set out on our difficult journey.

We are now ready to undertake the very last leg of our journey. We have already mentioned the rather strange proclamation that occupies such a central position in our Birkas HaLevanah:

דוד מלך ישראל חי וקים.
Dovid, King of Israel, Lives and Endures!

Let us be honest with ourselves. It is a difficult concept, is it not? TaNaCh records very clearly that Dovid died. So what can we possibly mean when we say that he lives? And what about "endures"? I suppose it means that his "living" will continue forever, that it will carry on until the Messianic epoch. Somewhere, certainly not among the living since he already died long ago, there is a "living" Dovid whose existence will never be curtailed and who will be with us until his descendant, the actual the Melech HaMoshiach for whom we are all waiting, will come to us and bring us home.

What does it all mean? What can it all mean?

Do you, dear reader, see that we have already given the answer? Do you not agree that all that we have written in the last few chapters demands to be recognized as the answer?

What is that? It is that the Dovid who died in Shmuel lives on in Tehilim! Lives on and will endure.

The match is perfect; let us spell it out. The moon, which—as life is lived now—orbits the earth in an unbroken rhythm of waxing and waning, will one day become a constant source of light. Let us phrase it a little differently. The truth that is manifest in the sliver of light, which is all that we can apprehend when the moon is in its crescent state, will one day brighten the entire moon, but only when Moshiach will have come. Reflect a moment! We celebrate Rosh Chodesh, not at full moon when the moon appears at the moment of its greatest accomplishment, but when the first tiny sliver becomes visible. I think I know why. It is because the full moon is not really natural to our present pre-Messianic state. It is really no more than an earnest of things to come. Let us remember what we learned in note 14, that the full moon occurs precisely when the earth is actually *between* the moon and the sun. That is not an ideal state, and will be eliminated when the moon, in the fullness of time, will cease to be a satellite of earth and become once more the light-generating star that it was originally.

All this is the precise parallel of the Dovid HaMelech whom we have come to know a little better in the pages of this book. Take a glance back at chapter 11 and you will recall how we showed that, in contrast to the original Dovid HaMelech upon whom the *ru'ach gevurah* with which Shmuel had endowed him rested only sporadically, allowing for periods of distance and a proclivity to making errors in religious judgments (the equivalent of the waxing and waning moon), the Melech HaMoshiach will be constantly endowed with this spirit (the ultimate full moon of self-generating light) and live his entire life in the presence of the Ribono shel Olam.

Now, just as today's orbiting moon whose true reality is expressed when it appears to us as a crescent nevertheless allows us a peek into the future on the one night every month when it appears to us as full, so the imperfect, historical Dovid allows us a glimpse, even today, into the Messianic future. That future nestles in Sefer Tehilim. As we defined it earlier, Tehilim is a "Messianic" book. The Tehilim were composed when the divine spirit was upon Dovid. Even though, for the historic Dovid, those times were interspersed with periods of "darkness," while they did hold sway they partook of the same measure of inspiration as will be the constant state of the Melech HaMoshiach. In that sense, Sefer Tehilim is the equivalent of the full moon at the halfway mark of every month. Neither of them reflects an absolute truth in the here and now, but both of them hint at a more perfect future.

So Dovid "lives" among us. He lives among the pages of the Tehilim that have accompanied us throughout our *golus*. And he will "endure" because it will be with our Tehilim in our hands that we will go out to greet our Melech HaMoshiach.

דוד מלך ישראל חי וקים.

INTRODUCTION

1. For the purpose of this essay, I will assume that עוסק בתורה in this context refers to the Torah aspect involved in *songs and praises*. This interpretation avoids the need to assume a *machlokes* in this detail between the two Gemaras that we have now quoted. After I wrote this endnote, I discovered that the late R. Yonasan Shteiff (Chadashim Gam Yeshanim) preceded me in making this suggestion.

2. לך דמיה תהלה (Tehilim 65:2).

3. At this point you, dear reader, may want to take a peek at chapter 21, the final chapter of *Music Made in Heaven*. There I say that Tehilim were, in a certain sense, written in paradise. The ideas expressed in this introduction and in chapter 21 reinforce one another and together project a more complete picture.

ONE *Jumping for Salvation*

1. The minhag is recorded in Maseches Soferim ch. 20. I do not know whether this is the earliest reference.

2. בכל יום אחכה לו שיבא.

3. שלשה הן הכופרים בתורה.

4. See Mishnah, Yoma 8:6, that teaches that someone who was stricken with a bulimus on Yom Kippur is to be fed immediately. This kind of hunger is life threatening.

TWO *Gad, the Precursor of Eliyahu Hanavi*

1. I describe the request as radical because, as Ramban makes clear in BeMidbar 21:21, there had been no intention on Moshe Rabbeinu's part to have any of the Israelites settle in Ever HaYarden. Ramban assigns two reasons: the first, that Moshe thought it best that all the people would dwell together in one place; the second, that the promise that the land would be flowing with milk and honey applied only to the area that lay to the west of the Yarden. The request made by the tribes of Gad and Reuven suggested a disposition that had not been contemplated.

2. ראשית.

3. חלקת, *the portion of.*

4. See what we wrote in note 1 above. At this point we will consider the continuation of the Ramban that we quoted there. He explains how it could have been possible that Moshe Rabbeinu had planned to simply leave the east side of the Yarden uninhabited.

הלא תראה שאם לא בקשוהו ממנו בני גד ובני ראובן לא היה מניח שם אדם אלא שתהיה לחרבה וכן
שנוי בספרי (תבא רצט) לתת לך, פרט לעבר הירדן שנטלת מעצמך, ועוד אמרו רבותינו (במדב"ר ז ח)

בעשר קדושות, שאין עבר הירדן ראוי לבית המקדש ולשכון השכינה, וכן נראה בכתוב שאמר
(יהושע כב יט) ואך אם טמאה ארץ אחזתכם וגו'

When you study the *parashah* in Mattos, it is perfectly clear that if the two tribes had not made their request, Moshe Rabbeinu would not have left a single person on the east side of the Yarden and would have left it desolate....Moreover Bereishis Rabba 7:8 has this to say: Ever HaYarden does not have the required sanctity to have the Beis HaMikdash built in its borders. It is not an area in which the Shechinah would dwell. This is evident from Yehoshua 22:19, where the tribes in Eretz Yisrael proper told the two and a half tribes, *if the land which you chose for yourself is unclean in your mind...*"

The reference to Yehoshua 22:19 is particularly significant and revealing about how the tribes felt about the eastern side of the Yarden, The background as recounted there is as follows. After Reuven and Gad, accompanied now by half the tribe of Menasheh, returned to the east bank, they immediately built an altar there. When this became known in Eretz Yisrael proper, it was construed as an act that would inevitably lead to idolatry. There was even a thought that it would be necessary to wage a civil war against the two and a half tribes, which seemed to be bent upon seceding from the Jewish people. It was only after the two and a half tribes explained that, on the contrary, they had built the altar in order to establish a more solid tie to their brethren to the west, that tempers cooled and tragedy was averted.

From all this it is very clear that the move by the two tribes was viewed with the utmost gravity and that it gave rise to grave suspicions that the entire thought process that made such a request possible indicated a wish to weaken their ties to Klal Yisrael and the Ribono shel Olam. It is understandable that Moshe Rabbeinu felt it necessary to put the whole matter into a more accurate light.

5. But see Sotah 13b.

6. It was a kindness of truly heroic proportions. We must recall that Leah's hope that she could somehow win Yaakov's love had been constantly frustrated. She called each of her first three sons by names that expressed the hope that with this birth there would finally be a breakthrough and that the disappointments engendered by the unfortunate circumstances of Lavan's perfidy might finally have dissipated and that the past could now be forgotten. It never happened. Even later, at the birth of her sixth son, Zevulun, she still expressed the hope that now, at last, Yaakov would make his permanent home with her (Bereishis 30:19).

If the repeated dashing of her hopes would have resulted in a degree of bitterness, we would have understood it perfectly. The fact that she was still capable of the altruistic sensitivity required to bring another competitor into the already tension-ridden household speaks much for the lofty personality of our mother, Leah.

7. See also Ramban at Bereishis 30:9.

8. See Bereishis Rabba 98:15: *They left their children as youngsters and returned to find them grown up. A child who was ten when his father left for war would now be twenty-four.*

9. In this instance, Reuven of course deserves as much praise as does Gad. However, this essay, for reasons that will become apparent immediately, focuses specifically upon Gad's place in our Jewish history. Actually, our thoughts about Reuven's mother, Leah, in note 6 can serve as an important beginning for tracing the sources of Reuven's altruism.

10. See Yechezkel 36:20.

THREE *The Monarchy*

1. I Shmuel, chapter 8, lists these prerogatives among those to which a king is entitled.

FOUR *Shaul's Downfall Is Rooted in His Perfection*

1. The Ramban that we quoted earlier suggests that, had Shaul not failed in his kingly duties, he would indeed have remained "king" but not in the fullest sense of the word. His hegemony would have been limited to a few of the tribes, perhaps Binyomin, Ephraim, and Menasheh, or he would have functioned in a subordinate role under the direction of a king from Yehudah.

2. See Esther Rabbah 7:8. Haman tried to persuade Mordechai to bow before him. After all, Mordechai's grandfather (Yaakov) had bowed before Haman's grandfather (Eisav) as recounted in *parashas* VaYishlach. Mordechai refused to accept this argument. His grandfather (Binyomin) had not yet been born at that time. In *his* family there was no tradition of groveling in front of Eisav/Amalek.

3. But see Yerushalmi Bikurim 3:3, which maintains that Shaul was like a year-old infant, not in the sense that he had never sinned but because one who becomes a king has all his sins *forgiven* on the day of his investiture.

4. I have not really answered the question as I formulated it above. I was disturbed why just the pure Shaul, who had never even dreamed of seeking the kingship, should have been burdened with a thankless task that could only end in disappointment.

   I relegate my suggested answer to the endnotes because I do not have the courage to offer it as part of the essay.

   Here is my suggestion.

   In Sefer Yechezkel, chapter 24, we read a shocking story. Yechezkel is told that God is about to take his beloved wife from him. That very evening she will die of the plague. Her death and her bereaved husband's mourning practices are to be a metaphor for the people of what will happen to them when the Beis HaMikdash is destroyed.

   The details of what all this involved need not detain us here. Since I first learned this passage, I have been plagued by a problem that has left me no rest. It is this: what can possibly be the justification for taking an innocent life in order to provide the people with a graphic lesson? I have never seen any Chazal that claims that this woman had in any way been sinful, such that she deserved to die at that particular moment.

Apparently people who have the responsibility of educating Klal Yisrael must be willing to bring even the ultimate sacrifice. If the Jews in those tragic years needed a graphic metaphor, then a woman of the stature to be Yechezkel's wife would have been willing to lay down her life in order to provide it.

Perhaps such was also Shaul's obligation. It was a sad duty that he had to undertake. It cost him dearly in a broken life. God demands much from His beloved tzadikim.

5. See Menachos 109b. תניא אמר ר' יהושע בן פרחיה בתחלה כל האומר עלה לה אני כופתו ונותנו לפני הארי עתה כל האומר לי לירד ממנה אני מטיל עליו קומקום של חמין שהרי שאול ברח ממנה וכשעלה בקש להרוג את דוד. R. Yehoshua ben Perachiah taught: "Originally before I became a *nasi*, I would have thrown anybody to the lions who suggested that I should become a *nasi*. Now that I am a prince, I would pour a kettle of boiling water over anybody who would want to persuade me to give up my position."

6. The commentators mention Rus as Dovid's "box of worms." In the light of all we know about her greatness, it seems strange that descent from her should have been viewed as a question mark hovering over Dovid's kingship. I do not know why these commentators make no mention of Lot and his daughters.

7. See, for example, Rashi to Tehilim 50:20, דופי דבר גנאי לדחותו לשון יהדפון. *Dofi* describes any disgrace. It is related to יהדפנו, *to push off a high place* (see commentators to BeMidbar 35:20). It is clear from the context of the Tehilim passage that general faults, not problems in one's lineage, are meant. We might also point to דברנו דופי in the אשמנו confession.

FIVE *At the Cradle of the Dovidic Kingship*

1. Please see Preface. My colleague feels that the sources do not necessarily yield this conclusion.

2. There are other commentators who prefer to have Shmuel referring to Shaul. According to them Eliav was short and ugly and, in Shmuel's eyes, was unsuited to be king. Shmuel assumed that God would now have to rescind His rejection of Shaul. He called out, "Surely [Shaul] His [already] anointed one is [now still] standing before God!"

3. Who, of course is Shmuel himself. See Bava Basra 14b. However there is a vast difference between Shmuel speaking as one of the actors in the drama and Shmuel as the divinely inspired narrator of Kisvei HaKodesh which, since it is part of Nevi'im, was surely written in the spirit of prophecy.

4. ולו היה בן ושמו שאול בחור וטוב ואין איש מבני ישראל טוב ממנו משכמו ומעלה גבה מכל העם.

5. י' קבין יופי ירדו לעולם ט' נטלה ירושלים כמ"ש בקדושין [מ"ט ב'] היינו דעיקר היופי דגוף אינו

אלא במקום שלימות היראה, *Ten measures of beauty descended upon the world, Yerushalayim appropriated nine of them. This is to be understood upon the basis that true physical beauty grows out of God fearing self abnegation.*

This idea is one of those which appear throughout the writings of this great Chasidic master. If you happen to own my book on Yerushalayim, *Harpstrings and Heartstrings*, you might want to look at chapter 10 where I elaborate on this theme.

SIX   *Florid—Though With Beautiful Eyes*

1. I have chosen to render אדמוני *florid,* rather than *ruddy,* because it seems to me from the dictionaries I have consulted that florid carries more of the sense of aggressiveness that, as will become evident in our analysis, is germane to the correct understanding of this sentence.

2. See Berachos 58a, which states that six hundred thousand scholars used to attend Yishai's lectures.

3. This is particularly surprising when we consider that Yishai's greatness of soul was itself an active factor in the choice of just one of *his* sons as king. See R. Tzadok HaKohen, Resisei Lailoh, Divrei Chalomos 18. כי בחירת דוד היתה מצד מעלת עצמו וגם מצד אביו וכמבואר מלשון הכתוב כי ראיתי בבניו לי מלך דמבואר דוקא של ישי מבניו באחד הי' למלך דהבחירה, *For the choice of Dovid came about both because of his own great stature and because of the stature of his father as can be seen from the language of the verse,* FOR I HAVE DETERMINED THAT MY KING WILL COME FROM AMONG HIS CHILDREN (I Shmuel 16:1). *This makes clear that the king could be chosen only from among Yishai's children.*

4. We shall document this in the coming chapter.

5. אדמוני **עם** יפה עינים.

6. This depends upon how to understand אדמוני. If it is a healthy reddish glow, then "together with" would be appropriate. The beautiful eyes augmented the charming complexion. If, however, אדמוני is to be taken as a florid complexion denoting anger and an aggressive nature, then the beautiful eyes come as a surprise. See note 1.

7. I owe the reader an explanation. On what basis does one "choose" a Malbim over a Radak? Clearly for me it does not involve an opinion concerning the objective value of one of the two alternatives. However, I had a number of considerations. In the first place, as you will see if you stick with me through this book, the idea of inner conflict within Dovid's personality is a (or perhaps *the*) staple of the picture I intend to paint. It is based on R. Tzadok's interpretation of why God refused Dovid permission to build the Beis HaMikdash, a subject to which we will come later on in the following chapter. As we go along you will see how basic this concept is to much of what we will be learning about Dovid HaMelech. All this is implied in the Malbim's translation but not in the Radak's.

   Then there is the preference that I suppose we all feel, to avoid irregular meanings. We have all been taught from childhood that עם is to be translated as the preposition *with* and not as the conjunction *and*. Of course the Radak would probably agree and was still willing to go with *and* on the basis of his interpretation of the Nachum phrase. I do not know whether the Radak could have adduced other places in TaNaCh for עם as *and* but the fact is that he did not. I looked up the Nachum phrase and found that Radak quotes our Shmuel phrase to bolster his interpretation there. Rashi, however, who is silent here, takes the עם in Nachum as *with* and that seems to make it likely that here he would agree with Malbim.

In general, I would assume that when a word is used irregularly, there must be some rationale. In our case we would have to have some explanation why the simple conjunctive ו"יו could not have been used and also what shading of עם as *with* would make it appropriate to make it stand in as *and* in our and the Nachum contexts. I have tried to think of an explanation but, to date, have not been successful. It is also surprising that in I Shmuel, chapter 17, as part of the Golias drama, the same irregularity appears once more (verse 42).

For these reasons it seemed to me legitimate to go with Malbim's interpretation and use it as a basis throughout the book for our analysis of the Dovidic saga.

SEVEN *Dovid and The Beis Hamikdash*

1. Devarim 12:10 lays down the rule (codified by Rambam, Melachim 1:2) that the obligation to build the Beis HaMikdash begins only after all of Israel's enemies had been vanquished and consequently a state of tranquillity had been attained. In Dovid's view, such was indeed the situation at that time.

    I have examined this episode in great detail in my Divrei HaYamim commentary (Mesorah Publications, Brooklyn, NY, 1987), volume 1, section 2, page 436. The analysis that I offer there can substantively augment the ideas with which we deal in this chapter.

2. As the story is told in Shmuel and in Divrei HaYamim, it is clear that the obligation to build the Beis HaMikdash falls primarily upon the king. However, Ramban (BeMidbar 16:21) asserts that the initiative could also have come from the people. Had this happened, Dovid would not have been disqualified. This is so because then he would have functioned entirely on the people's behalf and his personal disqualifications would not have interfered in carrying out *their* mandate.

3. There are major differences between the two accounts. I have discussed the disparate approaches to the story that are represented in the two books and explain those differences, in the essay that is referenced in note 1.

4. In the Ramban referenced above in note 2, Ramban explains this reason with the following words: והוא איש משפט ומחזיק במדת הדין ולא הוכשר בבית הרחמים, *Since he was a man prone to judgment, guided [in his actions] by the attribute of justice, he was not fit for [the task of building] the House of Mercy.*

5. This paragraph is a précis of R. Tzadok's thinking upon which he elaborates in Tzidkas HaTzadik 244.

6. R. Tzadok contrasts what we know concerning the sleeping habits of Dovid and Shlomo. After he quotes Succah 26b, which asserts that Dovid never slept longer than "the sleep of a horse (= sixty breaths)," he writes, ושלמה המע"ה אדרבא ישן הרבה ועליו נאמר כן יתן לידידו שנה, *By contrast, Shlomo slept a great deal. The verse,* כן יתן לידידו שנא, THUS WILL HE GRANT SLEEP TO HIS BELOVED, *refers to Shlomo.* (It is particularly interesting that this verse in Tehilim 127 is headed, שיר המעלות לשלמה, and contemplates the involvement of the Ribono shel Olam in the building of the Beis HaMikdash.) R. Tzadok's intention is to illustrate that Dovid, the tireless fighter, could not afford to allow himself to relax. Only after his constant struggles had yielded Shlomo's peaceful reign was it possible for Shlomo to permit himself ample sleep.

I believe that only the relationship between Dovid and Shlomo can explain the unique occurrence of which we are taught in II Shmuel 12:24–25, *Dovid comforted Bas Sheva, approached her and lay with her and she bore a son. She called him Shlomo* AND HASHEM LOVED HIM. *God sent a message by the hands of Nathan the prophet* AND HE CALLED [THE BABY] YEDIDYAH IN HASHEM'S BEHALF.

To the best of my knowledge there is no other case in which the Ribono shel Olam "loved" a newborn baby. We can understand that the Ribono shel Olam would "love" a great and holy tzadik. But why love a newborn who has had no time at all to earn any merits? And why actually call this baby "Beloved of God" at this early stage in his life?

None of this presents a problem if we see Shlomo as a continuation of Dovid's heroic life. The baby Shlomo was none other than "Dovid" cleansed of all the negative traits that had so plagued him in the past. Such a child, the tangible outgrowth of a life of battles bravely waged, one could indeed love even in infanthood.

7. We will be analyzing the Bas Sheva incident later in this book.

EIGHT *Shepherds As Judges*

1. In chapter 3, I paraphrased this final phrase as *will be entirely fair*. In the present chapter, where our interest will be focused upon the *justice* that the Ribono shel Olam will administer, I have translated literally.

2. והריחו.

3. צפית לישועה?

4. והריחו.

5. והריחו ביראת ה'.

6. וירח ה' את ריח הניחוח (Bereishis 8:21).

7. לפי שהריח היא הרגשה קלה. I suppose he means that when we smell something the sensation travels straight to the brain and does not (at least to our perception) require the type of processing that involves bodily functions as when we experience taste, sight, or touch.

8. מורח ודאין.

9. אור שברא הקדוש ברוך הוא ביום ראשון אדם צופה בו מסוף העולם ועד סופו.

10. I have taken the Chagigah passage metaphorically. The Chazal obviously deals with סתרי תורה and I am, of course, aware that of these I know nothing at all. Nevertheless, it seems to me that since it is included in the Gemara there must be a *p'shat* level at which this *mesorah* can be meaningful to us.

11. The *sugia* in Mo'ed Katan deserves much fuller treatment than I am able to give it within the confines of this book. A good start for the interested reader is the late Rav Hutner's Pachad Yitzchak on Yom Kippur, chapter 11.

NINE *The Dovid of Shmuel and the Dovid of Tehilim*

1. Here is a flashing amber light. I do not mean to convey the idea that any part of TaNaCh is to be viewed as a simple history text book. I use the term "historical account" merely to contrast Sefer Shmuel with Sefer Tehilim, which, as we shall see further along in this book, deals with essence rather than with form.

2. This section is reproduced by permission of the family. Dr. Biberfeld ז"ל, a chemist by profession, was, like his father, Dr. Edouard Biberfeld ז"ל (author of מנוחה נכונה on הלכות שבת), an outstanding example of the Hirschian educational philosophy. The book from which our quotation is taken is a masterful study of Dovid HaMelech and it was his pioneering work that inspired me to try my hand at taking it a little further. I owe a great deal to his insights.

3. Note that the author speaks of "visions of harmony," not of harmony itself. See chapter 7, where we learned that true harmony escaped Dovid during his lifetime and was achieved only at the moment of his death.

4. I am not sure what the author means by "entirely." See our chapter 11, where we discuss whether the spirit with which Dovid was imbued at the time of his investiture was permanent or sporadic.

5. Who is the author of II Shmuel. See Bava Basra 14b.

6. An example would be the third psalm, which, according to its heading, was composed as Dovid was fleeing from his rebellious son, Avsholom. That tragic story is told in all its stark horror in II Shmuel, chapters 15 and 16. It seems to me that mention of Dovid's contemplation of the transience of evil and the firm belief in ultimate vindication would have added much to the understanding of this episode.

Herewith a quote from Biberfeld in his *David, King of Israel*, in which he grapples with the problem that the text of psalms the headings of which tie them to specific events, never describe the actual event with which they are associated.

Even those psalms which according to their headings owe their existence to certain events in David's life *never refer in their contents to those events.*

No stronger formal indication of the timelessness of the psalms could be imagined.

The reason is clear. To David every event spelled its eternal meaning; nature and history could not conceal their immutable core of truth. Without hesitation, without perceptible effort, every concrete event was, in his soul, traced to its timeless essence. The treacherous inhabitants of Ziff appear as evil incarnate. Doeg the Edomite as the cruelty of man to man personified...whatever event, grievous or joyous, occurred in his life, was in his meditation recast in the mold of eternity. Hence the immediacy and directness with which the psalms appeal to man. They speak of what moves man's heart at all times and places, of everrecurring human problems divorced of the incidentals of place and time. The psalms are forever alive. Through them David speaks to every Jew in every age. The David of the psalms is the David of the present.

TEN *A Closer Look at Sefer Shmuel*

1. תורה היא וללמוד אנו צריכים, borrowed from Berachos 62a where it is used in the singular, וללמוד אני צריך.

2. I am the author of Mesorah Publication's Divrei HaYamim and, as part of the commentary to that book I make extensive comparisons between the historiography of the two books as also of the different language which they often employ in describing the same events. If you, dear reader, want a more complete picture of Dovid HaMelech than is possible within the limits of this small book, I would recommend that you take a look at the Divrei HaYamim commentary,

3. To understand what I mean by this, we should turn to Sanhedrin 34a. That passage deals with a cryptic verse in Tehilim 62:12, אחת דבר אלהים שתים זו שמ־עתי, *One thing God has spoken; two things have I heard*. From this the gemara derives that, מקרא אחד יוצא לכמה טעמים, *one verse can be utilized to express many different ideas*.. Every piece of writing, certainly every piece of writing in *kisvei hakodesh*, has a body and a soul.

   It is for this reason that p'shat and d'rash are what they are. P'shat, from פשט, to spread out and hence, to be readily accessible, is that meaning of the text which springs out at the reader at the initial scanning. The words carry their most natural meaning; the grammar of form and syntax obeys the rules and does not grate upon our sensibilities. The information which is conveyed is thoroughly at home in the context in which it appears, and what is said is not contradicted by any of the other assumptions which are made by the passage

   D'rash, on the other hand, derives from דרש, to search for something. The text will not yield these treasures on a first reading. They must be the fruits of a strong identity beween the author and the reader. The two must occupy one thought-world, one heart must animate them both, one mind must be open to the promptings of that heart. Once such an identity has been established, then, as between two loving friends a hint or a wink can tell entire stories, so that the fourth dimension of every written word will be laid bare.

4. I have used "poetic composition" rather than "psalm" since this piece has no parallel in the Book of Psalms.

5. See note 4 in the following chapter. There, I offer a possibility for solving this riddle.

6. .וידבר דוד ליהוה את דברי השירה הזאת ביום הציל יהוה אתו מכף כל איביו ומכף שאול

7. Abarbanel explains the many minor changes between the Tehilim version and that which appears in Sefer Shmuel by maintaining that the wording in Shmuel fit Dovid's unique personality and his own experiences best. When he included it with the other psalms in Tehilim, thus making it available to the public, he made appropriate changes..

8. See below on II Shmuel 23:1: ונעים זמירות ישראל. I believe that the rendering which I have offered here., expresses the simple meaning of this phrase.

9. At this point, I want to include a segment from another essay which I wrote for this book, but which I then decided for various reasons not to include. The segment which I will quote here deals with two issues: It reflects upon the fact that Dovid's kingship is said to be compared to the moon (see Introduction) and also why a number of people looked upon Dovid as a mal'ach, an angel.

Perhaps another aspect of the comparison lies in the fact that the moon has absolutely no light of its own. For us earthlings the moon exists only to the extent that the sun shines upon it. It has what it is given and nothing more. The picture of the moon would thus be an accurate portrayal of the mal'ach as we have understood him. He has absolutely no personality of his own, exists only as the embodiment of the task for which the Ribono shel Olam created him. Dovid HaMelech's throne, his kingship, has no personal dimension. It defines his essence as surely and as accurately as the mal'ach's task defines him.

This may also be implied by another midrashic tradition which appears in various forms in diverse Aggadic contexts. The Ribono shel Olam told Adam that one day Dovid was to be born but that he had no years of life allotted to him. Adam volunteered to give Dovid seventy years of his own life. Now whatever else the midrash might be teaching us, it is clear that Dovid was to have no existence which he would be able to call his own. He lived only for the time that it took him to fulfill whatever task had been assigned to him through the life-span that had been gifted to him by Adam.

Once we have learned to regard Dovid in this very special way, other aspects of his life come to mind which take on a new and up until now unsuspected coloration. In at least two instances Dovid describes himself as personifying a quality or an action. For example, in Tehilim 109:4 he proclaims, "I am [a man (or personification) of] prayer." Again, in

Tehilim 120:7 he says of himself, "I am [a man (or personification) of] peace." Now we have softened the impact of these two phrases by inserting brackets and parentheses. However, the text as it stands is much more direct: "I am prayer," I am peace." This locution implies precisely what it says. "I am the embodiment of prayer or peace. My entire being is suffused by these qualities or actions. There are no hidden nooks within my personality to which prayer or the search for peace does not penetrate. I am nothing but a praying or peace-loving being." This ties in well with the point which we have made that Dovid's was the single-dimensional personality of the mal'ach. When he prayed he was only prayer, when in pursuit of peace he was nothing other than a quest for peace.

10. I am not entirely sure that the wording which I am using here is correct. It supposes that Sefer Shmuel purports to be the story of Dovid HaMelech. That may not be the case any more than, let us say, Sefer Yehoshua is the story of Yehoshua. I sense that in general we look at these books as being concerned with something broader than the lives of their central figures. I simply do not know enough to have an opinion on this issue.

11. Tehilim 109:4, ואני תפלה.

12. Tehilim 120:7, אני שלום.

13. See the final paragraph in endnote 9.

14. The interplay between Sefer Shmuel and Sefer Tehilim comes into sharp play in the story of Dovid's teshuvah in the matter of Bas Sheva (see II Shmuel 12:13). Noson HaNovi's chastisement is fierce and uncompromising, especially v. 12: *For you acted in secret but I will punish you in public for all of Israel to see.* Dovid's reaction shocks in both its simplicity and its complexity. In Shmuel we have the simple, חטאתי לה', *I have sinned before HaShem.* There are no excuses and no explanations which would tend towards some kind of justification or at least mitigation. It seems to me that without the knowledge imparted to us by Tehilim, that Dovid was the personification of prayer, which means that every moment of his life he stood humbly before his God, such heroism would have been entirely beyond our comprehension. As it is, nothing surprises. If one lives constantly with God then there is no alternative to the unadorned truth. And then there is the complexity. Tehilim 51, the psalm which he composed when Noson Hanovi came to him with his devastating criticism, provides it. It reveals to us the depth of feeling and experience which animated the modest two-word declaration which we have in Shmuel.

15. For this expression, see Sanhedrin 42a and more particularly, Rashi there.

ELEVEN *Dovid's "Final Words"*

1. I have not been consistent in choosing the various fillers which I offered in my translation. I simply chose from among the ideas offered by various commentators, with no other objective than to present a reasonably readable passage.

2. Perhaps that is a question which we ought not to be asking. Perhaps, in asking it we are crossing some red line beyond which we ought not venture. But then again, we are learning the Torah which the Ribono shel Olam wants us to study to the very best of our abilities. Perhaps He will help us reach a truth if we hunger enough for understanding the precious gift which He has given us.

3. ‏ואלה דברי דוד האחרונים.

4. I imagine that each of the four qualities which Dovid enumerates here would have contributed to his ability to express the delight of Israel's songs. Herewith a short explanation for each one:

   1. Dovid ben Yishai: Shabbos 55b lists Yishai among the four people who died only because of the "wily cunning of the snake (in Eden)." That is, that they were completely without any sins of their own. See Maharal Chidushei Aggada to that Gemara.

   2. Of him who was raised on high: Against all expectations, Dovid had been taken from the sheepfold and anointed king. Clearly he must have been uniquely qualified. Rambam (Melachim 3:6) teaches that the king's heart "is the heart of the entire people." This identification with Klal Yisrael made him more suited than any other to give voice to the music which resonated with the people.

   3. I Shmuel 16:13 reports that when Shmuel anointed Dovid, he was imbued with a *ru'ach HaShem*, a Godly spirit. Rashi identifies this spirit as imbuing him with power (*ru'ach gevurah*) while the Targum renders *ru'ach nevu'ah*, a spirit of prophecy. Radak accepts both and explains that the *ru'ach gevurah* made it possible for Dovid to kill Golias and to protect his father's flocks by destroying a lion and a bear (I Shmuel 17:34). The *ru'ach nevu'ah*, on the other hand, describes the spirit of prophecy which enabled Dovid to compose his songs and his psalms.

   4. The moment that Shmuel anointed Dovid was the moment that Dovid became *he who lends delights to Israel's songs*.

5. Please see Preface. My colleague feels that the sources do not yield this conclusion.

6. Please see Preface. My colleague feels that the sources do not yield this conclusion.

7. In the previous chapter we wondered why Sefer Shmuel cites none of the psalms which, as indicated by many of the headings in Sefer Tehilim, were said on occasions which are recounted in Sefer Shmuel. We left that question unanswered.

   Our thoughts in the present chapter, to the extent that they might be correct, may provide an answer. Sefer Shmuel may have been composed with the view of presenting Dovid's life as it was actually lived. As a matter of fact, his life was punctuated by periods of distance from the Ribono shel Olam, which would not allow room for the inspiration which expressed itself in the psalms.

   I would like to formulate this thought as follows: in the previous chapter

I noted that telling the stories while leaving out the psalms to which they gave birth is presenting only half, and therefore an untrue, picture. As I am writing now, it seems to me that that untrue picture has an element of truth in it. The periods of distance which were a part of Dovid's reality, are only untrue when we speak about the total picture of his life. On the ground, as they occurred, they were very true. Indeed, Sefer Shmuel describes them as they were.

8. מהיום ההוא ומעלה.

9. Such as the killing of the lion and the bear, or, indeed, of Golias, or the moments when he felt called upon to compose a psalm.

10. ותצלח.

11. צלח.

12. עבר.

13. וצלחו הירדן.

14. ועבר עליו רוח קנאה.

15. מנוחה from נוח as in נחה.

TWELVE *Dovid Remains In Yerushalayim*

1. The interested reader can find such an analysis in my commentary on Divrei HaYamim, already mentioned (part of the ArtScroll TaNaCh series published by Mesorah Publications).

THIRTEEN *An Ill-fated Gesture of Kindness*

1. Rashi cites a midrash that teaches that when Dovid was fleeing from Shaul he brought his family to the Moabite king for protection. Far from helping them, the Moabite king slaughtered them all except for one brother who escaped to Ammon. The Ammonite king welcomed him and protected him. It was this kindness that Dovid now wanted to repay.

2. Radak points out that the אל here is to be understood as though it were written על.

3. See the Kesef Mishneh cited above. He asks this same question on his own explanation of Dovid's justification.

4. רצוי rather than מחוייב.

FOURTEEN *Dovid's State of Mind Made Him Prone to Error*

1. See Bereishis Rabbah 63:3, that each one of the Avos was "called" Yisrael.

2. Although Moshe Rabbeinu is frequently referred to in midrashic literature as being כנגד ששים רבוא, *the equivalent of six hundred thousand* (cf. Shir HaShirim Rabba 1:65), that is not the same as saying that the entire nation is, so to speak, contained in him. That, however, is the case of the Avos.

3. See Rashi, BeMidbar 21:21, שמשה הוא ישראל וישראל הם משה לומר לך שנשיא הדור הוא הכל כי הנשיא הוא ככל הדור, *for Moshe is Yisrael and Yisrael is Moshe, because the*

prince "is" everything. See also, Rambam Melachim 3:6, שלבו הוא לב כל ישראל, *for his heart is the heart of all Israel.* This of course stands in contradiction to what I wrote in the previous endnote. At this moment I cannot offer an explanation for the fact that Moshe Rabbeinu never attained the level at which the Ribono shel Olam would have referred to Himself as אלהי משה.

FIFTEEN *An Afternoon Stroll*

1. See Tehilim 86:2, שמרה נפשי כי חסיד אני, *Preserve my soul for I am a* CHASID.
2. Maharal uses the word טיול, the equivalent of a pleasure trip. It is because of Ramban's choice of words that I translated מתהלך as "strolling." An air of relaxation permeates the whole story.
3. לולי תורתך שעשועי, Tehilim 119:92.
4. זמירות היו לי חוקיך, Tehilim 119:54.
5. The expression ראויה משמת ימי בראשית conveys much more than extreme antiquity. It means that the necessity of this particular union was woven inextricably into the very fabric of history.

SIXTEEN *Strange Encounters*

1. We recall that the only hunters in TaNaCh are Eisav and Nimrod.
2. Distasteful because Bas Sheva was expecting to be reunited with her husband, Uriah the Hittite. In the course of our discussion we will be learning from Chazal that while Uriah was at the front, Bas Sheva was not formally married to him. It was customary for the soldiers to divorce their wives before they went out to battle, so that their wives would not experience any complications if the husbands were not to return from the war. Nevertheless, since the expectation was certainly that her husband would come back, Bas Sheva was, at the very least emotionally, tied to Uriah.
3. See Sanhedrin 19b, that Boaz's self-control under these circumstances is ranked higher than that of Yosef who withstood the blandishments of Potiphar's wife.
4. We will offer some ideas in the following chapter.

SEVENTEEN *Yehudah and Tamar I*

1. See Chizkuni who points out that the word אֶל is occasionally used instead of the prefix ב, meaning *in.*
2. The story begins with the words וירד יהודה, *Yehudah went down.* Chazal understand this to mean, *Yehudah was forced downward,* that is, he was deposed from his position of kingship.
3. They are: 1. Why does Rashi have to suggest a second explanation? and 2. Why did he not do so in the earlier Rashi that we quoted above? Maharal, in Gur Aryeh, tackles them both.
4. The full verse reads, *For I know the thoughts that I am thinking, says HaShem,*

thoughts of peace leading to no evil, thoughts that will give you an end to which you can look forward with hope.

5. Dovid's lineage is traced back to Peretz, one of the twins whom Tamar bore to Yehudah, in Rus 4:18.

6. When the Ribono shel Olam told Avraham that at some time in the future his children would be slaves in a foreign land, that land is not identified. It is called simply *a land that is not theirs.* We learn that that land was Mitzraim only at the beginning of Sefer Shemos.

EIGHTEEN *Yehudah and Tamar II*

1. In the *sefarim* which are available to me. I have not been able to find very extensive discussions of this phenomenon. Only two explanations were brought to my attention. After I will have explained both of them briefly, I will point out why I found both of them less than totally satisfying.

The first makes use of the concept שוחד לשטן, literally, *a bribe offered to Satan.* This idea is based upon the assumption that when great and holy things are about to happen, Satan, whose task it is to fight against all that is good and holy, will make enormous efforts to frustrate the hoped for results. At such a time it is said to be useful to extend what appears to be a small victory to Satan—in effect a bribe—which will satisfy his lust and persuade him to desist from his destructive activities. A good place to study this concept is the Michtav MeiEliyahu of Rav Dessler, volume I, page 262. Rav Dessler asserts that the concept is found frequently in Chazal, particularly in the Zohar. My search program did not turn up a single instance in which the words "שוחד לשטן" are used and I must assume that Rav Dessler did not mean the particular term but the idea which energizes it.

Now I have not been able to find any Rishon who uses this concept to explain the difficulties attendant upon the establishment of the monarchy with which we are struggling here. It is used by שמואל די אוזירא in his commentary אגרת שמואל, to Megilas Rus printed in the TaNaCh published by the Pardes Publishing House Inc. My good friend R. Noson Sherman uses it in his Overview to the Megilas Rus which was published by Mesorah Publications. In his essay he mentions that this explanation appears in the Chafetz Chaim on Torah. Beyond these, I have not been able to find it being used in our context.

Another possibility was pointed out to me by my good friend, Rabbi Abba Tzvi Naiman. Yoma 22b asserts that no leadership position should be filled by anyone who does not have a "box of worms" hanging on his back. The gemara explains that unless there is something unsavory in the leader's background, there is a strong possibility that he will become conceited and overbearing. Rashi explains that the "box of worms" is a metaphor for a less than perfect family background; in the case of Dovid HaMelech it would be his descent from the Moabite Rus.

Perhaps, then, this could explain the apparently ugly means by which the royal line of Dovid was brought forth. The ambiguous circumstances under which significant pairings took place, would supply the ideal "box of worms".

My hesitation to accept either of these two possibilities lies in the fact that neither of them suggests an intrinsic relationship between the kingship and the questionable incidents which lay along the road of its realization. They do no more than suggest peripheral advantages which accrued. The Satan would be bought off and the kings of the royal line would have their potential conceit punctured. It seems to me that both these considerations are too weak to carry the burden of the enormous difficulties which confound us. I believe that the idea which I will present in the essay, does a more thorough job than either of the other two.

2. We are told only that she was the daughter of a "Canaanite" man. Ramban, based on Targum, makes the point that this does not mean that the woman came from a Canaanite lineage. We know from the story of Ytzchak's marriage to Rivka that in the home of our patriarchs marriage to the accursed Canaanite nation was considered to be an abomination.

Ramban makes the point that even at the simple *p'shat* level it seems unlikely that the lineage was meant. This story took place in Canaan and so a Canaanite lineage could have been taken for granted. Rather Targum and, in his footsteps, Ramban take the word to mean a peddler or merchant (which means that in the first line of this endnote I should not have capitalized the "c" of "Canaanite). We know the usage of 'Canaani" as *peddler* from Mishley 31 (Eishes Chayil), וחגור נתנה לכנעני.

3. Please see Preface. My colleague feels that the sources do not yield this conclusion.

4. I used my search program to see what I could find about this term in the literature. I found occasional reference to the term in various books on the kabalah but could understand nothing of what was being said. I consulted with a friend who is more conversant in the kabalah literature than I am, whether, in as much as the subject was being discussed in kabalah, there was any justification in suggesting a meaning, as I am about to do within, which is simply an attempt to explain things on the *p'shat* level, but which surely has nothing to do with the ideas which are discussed in that literature. He felt that there was no problem at all and it is on the basis of his advice, that I will offer my ideas.

5. I am assuming that "day", in this context, need not be limited to a twenty-four hour period. R. Yitzchok Isaac HaLevi in his Doros HaRishonim proves this from the expression אותו היום, which the Mishnah uses to describe the "day" when the *nesi'us* passed from Rabban Gamliel to R. Elazar ben Azaeiah. The amount of legislation which is said to have taken place on that "day" is so huge that a much larger period of time must have been meant.

6. An endnote is different and, perhaps, allows for a moment of conjecture. I believe that since 1948 we all have indeed lived in a time that can be de-

scribed as לא יום ולא לילה. There have been such enormous gifts and such enormous disappointments that attaching any kind of label to what has occurred seems to me to be truly impossible. Is it "day" or is it "night"? We all know that there are good Jews on either side of that particular conundrum. As I am writing this endnote in Benei Berak (פרשת וירא תשס"ז) with a dreadful parade scheduled this Friday in Yerushalayim, the possibility that we are entering a time that might be called, והיה לעת ערב, seems not at all impossible. May the Ribono shel Olam have mercy on all of us.

7. The Hebrew, ערב, for *evening* is formed from the root, ערב, *to mix things up together.* This is so because as evening falls and the daylight begins to dim, it becomes harder to identify objects or people correctly. The word לילה for *night* is derived from בלל, *to fuse two elements into one another completely,* such that they cannot be told apart at all.

NINETEEN *Dovid's Mistake*

1. For this last phrase, see above in chapter 15.

2. כל האומר דוד חטא אינו אלא טועה. We should note that this does not mean that Dovid had not sinned at all. Nathan *did* come to give him *musar* and, as we recall from chapters 8 and 10 (see particularly note 14 in chapter 10), Dovid became the very paradigm of the efficacy of sincere teshuvah. Chazal mean that he did not transgress the weighty sins that a superficial reading would have had us believe. His guilt lay in a different direction, as we shall soon see.

3. I mean that she was not bound to Uriah in a legal sense. Psychologically, they were still husband and wife in the sense that they had every intention of remarrying once Uriah returned from the battlefield. If this were not the case, then the parable of the sheep would not have been true.

4. In Tehilim 51:6, in which Dovid begs the Ribono shel Olam to forgive his sins in the Bas Sheva debacle, Dovid says לך לבדך חטאתי, *I have sinned only to you.* Many commentators read this phrase as meaning that it lay in God's power to forgive him since his sin was between him and God, not between him and man. He had not sinned against Uriah. I have tried to understand what the Rishonim, particularly Rashi, say about this, but was not able to be יורד לסוף דעתו.

   As I am suggesting the nature of Dovid's miscalculation, it could be explained as follows. If Dovid's understanding would have been correct, if indeed Bas Sheva would have been his Tamar, then he would have been in the right when he rode roughshod over Uriah's feelings. The Ribono shel Olam had shown him what He wanted and there was therefore no need to take anybody's feelings into consideration. In that case, Dovid could claim with a good conscience that he had not sinned against Uriah. In any other circumstance he would have been totally sensitive to his needs. In the situation as it was, it is true that he had harmed Uriah, but only because he had misunderstood God's intentions. He had therefore sinned to God but not to man.

TWENTY *Tying up Some Loose Ends*

1. The story of the relationship between Mipiboshes and Tziva and of Dovid's relationship to both of them is complex and spreads over a number of chapters. It begins with II Shmuel, chapter 9. Since our study of the Dovid/ Bas Sheva saga began with Dovid's ill-fated decision to send comforters to Chonun of Ammon, it is worth noting that the two stories are juxtaposed. The Mipiboshes story is told in chapter 9 and the Ammon debacle in chapter 10.

    One gets the impression that the two stories are connected. They occurred at a time when Dovid's kingship was firmly established and he seems to have judged that now was the time to mend fences with various people to whom he felt an obligation. His first effort was directed to Shaul's family (Mipiboshes); after that he turned to his Ammonite friends. I am not sure why it should have happened that both gestures ended in tragedy.

TWENTY-ONE *Dovid Is Alive and Will Endure*

1. For those of you who want to understand more of the background than I supply in the essay, I offer the following details. Maharal's thesis is based on the assumption that the people who lived sinless lives did so in the merit of either their father or their son. Binyomin would thus have attained his exalted level because of the merit of his father, Yaakov. Amrom made the grade because of his son, Moshe Rabbeinu. Now Maharal works out that both Yaakov and Moshe Rabbeinu had attained even higher levels of purity than would be expressed in the concept of having died because of the "wiles of the snake." Because of their higher level of sanctity they were able to pull up their son or their father to the requisite level.

    In the case of Yishai and Kil'ov, we cannot make this principle work by drawing on Dovid in the sense that he was Yishai's son and Kil'ov's father. As we now know, Dovid *had* failed on certain occasions. We know nothing special about either Yishai's father or Kil'ov's son. Accordingly, given the theory with which Maharal is working, we cannot understand how these two, Yishai and Kil'ov, attained the level they did.

    I repeat that I do not pretend to understand Maharal and draw on him only in the present instant, for the technical details that will help me to fulfill the task I have set myself.

2. At this point you might want to review chapter 6, particularly the Malbim's ideas about the instability Yishai feared and, as we worked it out, Shmuel was taught by the Ribono shel Olam to value.

3. Check back to chapter 11 where we discuss the difference between Dovid's initial anointment and the ultimate one that will imbue the Melech HaMoshiach with a divine spirit that will never, even for a moment, leave him.

4. שהקים עולה של תשובה. Taking על as though it were written עול, *yoke*, is perfectly permissible in the realm of דרש. However, changing the *hoph'al* הוקם into the *hiph'il* הקים might well raise eyebrows. There is obviously some significant depth involved here. I will attempt to tackle that in the essay.

5. See Tehilim 84, which Malbim maintains was composed in the Babylonian exile. The Levite who sings this psalm is full of hope that he will yet return to Eretz Yisrael and accompany the divine Temple service with his music. He sings this song in praise of those who faithfully continue to hope for salvation. He prays that the Temple might be restored and the Dovidic kingship reestablished. In verse 9, where the composer entreats God that his prayers might be answered he refers to Him as אלהי יעקב.

6. For the relationship between Yaakov and Yosef in the protection of the exiled Jews, see my book *The Riddle of the Bowing Moon*.

7. A caveat is in place. The thoughts that follow are my thoughts, not those of Henry Bieberfeld. I have no right to burden him with my idiosyncratic ideas. His role in what follows in this paragraph and in the rest of this essay is merely that his felicitous expression "the idea of God" stimulated my thinking.

8. חסד ומשפט אשירה.

9. You may want to study that whole *sugia* in Berachos there. The Gemara gives this theme a very thorough treatment.

10. See Sanhedrin 67b.

אם ישראל עושים תשובה נגאלין ואם לאו אין נגאלין אמר ליה רבי יהושע אם אין עושין תשובה אין נגאלין אלא הקדוש ברוך הוא מעמיד להן מלך שגזרותיו קשות כהמן וישראל עושין תשובה ומחזירן למוטב.

Rabbi Eliezer taught: Israel will be redeemed only if they do *teshuvah*. R. Yehoshua responded, "Will they only be redeemed if they do teshuvah, and if they do not do teshuvah they will not be redeemed? [How can that be?] [The truth is that if they do not do teshuvah] God will appoint a king over them whose decrees will be as harsh as those of Haman and [as a result] Israel will do teshuvah."

11. ויהי רצון מלפניך יהוה אלהי ואלהי אבותי למלאת פגימת הלבנה ולא יהיה בה שום מעוט. ויהי אור הלבנה כאור החמה וכאור שבעת ימי בראשית כמו שהיתה קדם מעוטה. שנאמר את שני המארות הגדולים. ויתקים בנו מקרא שכתוב ובקשו את יהוה אלהיהם ואת דויד מלכם. אמן.

12. Rashi bases his assertion upon Tehilim 89 where we have a phrase (spread over verses 37 and 38) that reads, כסאו כשמש נגדי כירח יכון עולם, *His throne is like the sun in My view, and like the moon will be established forever*. It is interesting that Rashi, in his commentary there, states simply that the sun and moon, which are constant presences in the sky, bear witness to the constancy of the Dovidic kingship. In this view there appears to be no indication that Dovid's kingship is in any way compared to the moon.

13. My search program turned up many ספרי קבלה that deal with the issue.

I would like here to quote a passage from *The Hirsch Siddur*, which I have also placed at the very beginning of this book. It comes from his commentary to Birkas HaLevanah:

According to Rosh HaShanah 25a, this was the code message by which Rabbi Yehudah HaNasi had asked Rabbi Chiya to notify him that he had fulfilled Kiddush HaChodesh with which he had been charged. For, of Dovid it is said, כירח יכון עולם ועד בשחק נאמן סלה (Tehilim 89:38). That even though the course of Dovid's life, like the course of the moon, would be a process of constant change, and that at times, like the moon, he might even seem to disappear from sight, Dovid, even as the moon which is eternal, nevertheless shall live and remain for all time. And even as the moon will always bear faithful testimony to God's mighty power in the skies above, so, Dovid, too, will ever remain a constant, loyal witness for God's rule and man's role and destiny upon the horizon of the nations.

14. Here is a little background to this paragraph. The first time I wrote it, I was sitting in a plane and did not have any encyclopedias available to me. In my innocence I had always thought that the reason why we cannot see parts of the moon at different times during the month is because they are blocked out by the earth. The formerly invisible sections of the moon become visible as it edges past the earth and makes itself accessible to the light of the sun.

If you are as ignorant as I was, you would have loved what I wrote—as I did when I wrote it—because it all works out so nicely. The earth (= earthiness = גשמיות) blocks out the healing rays of the sun as surely as sins block out the light of the Ribono shel Olam, and so on and so on.

I was smart enough to consult an encyclopedia when I got home and realized that I was completely wrong. There is not a single moment in the moon's orbit in which half of the moon is not illuminated by the sun. The same half is always lit; the other half is always dark because it does not face the sun. When all we see is a waxing or waning crescent it is not because only that much of the moon is lighted up. It is because at whatever moment we are discussing, the moon is positioned vis-à-vis the earth in such a way that only that part of the (unchanging) lighted half is visible to us. Contrary to what I had thought, we see the full moon precisely when the earth is positioned between the sun and the moon.

The paragraph you are reading is a rewrite of what I had originally done.

Now I am not sure what Ramo's idea was of this matter. He writes in Orech Chaim 426:2, in his discussion of the Birkas HaLevanah, which we perform every month, that *Kneses Yisrael will one day once more cleave to her husband, Who is the Ribono shel Olam, just like the moon which periodically establishes a new relationship with the sun....It is for this reason that we rejoice and dance during the Kidush HaChodesh just as though it were a wedding.*

That sounds very much as I had thought originally.

It seems to me that even if it is true that things do not happen in quite that way, we need not feel strange when we dance at the Kidush HaLevanah. Joy, after all, is a function of the way we feel and there is no doubt in my mind that we *experience* the various phases of the moon precisely as the Ramo describes them.

15. With all that this implies. See previous note.

IN RECOGNITION OF A

GENEROUS CONTRIBUTION

IN MEMORY

OF

Dr. Richard

&

Regina Weinberger

OF

VIENNA, AUSTRIA

AND

BALTIMORE, MARYLAND

IN MEMORY

OF

OUR BELOVED

HUSBAND, FATHER,

AND

TEACHER

Solomon Ralph Bijou

HE LIT A LIGHT IN OUR HEARTS

THAT

WILL GUIDE US AND OUR CHILDREN

THROUGHOUT OUR LIVES.

—FROM HIS WIFE,

CHILDREN, GRANDCHILDREN,

AND

GREAT-GRANDCHILDREN

IN LOVING MEMORY

OF

Esther & Isaac Mezrahi

PILLARS OF OUR COMMUNITY,

THEY ALWAYS KNEW WHAT HAD TO BE DONE

AND, PROFOUNDLY CREATIVE,

FOUND WAYS TO DO IT.

ABOVE ALL THEY WERE A TEAM.

ONE HEART

ANIMATED THEM BOTH,

ONE SOUL

BREATHED LIFE INTO THEIR DREAMS.

AFTER FATHER PASSED ON,

MOTHER KEPT THE FLAME BURNING

FOR EIGHTEEN MORE YEARS.

MAY THEIR MEMORY BE A BLESSING

FOR US, OUR CHILDREN, AND GRANDCHILDREN.

THERE ARE MANY PEOPLE

WHO OWE

THEIR LIVES

TO

THE LOVING CONCERN OF

Ezra & Zekia Shasho

OF BLESSED MEMORY.

WE GRATEFULLY RECALL THEIR GOODNESS

AND

THE WONDERFUL EXAMPLE THAT THEY SET.

THEY, AS ALSO

THEIR BELOVED DAUGHTER

Frieda Kredy

OF BLESSED MEMORY,

WILL FOREVER LIVE ON IN OUR HEARTS.

—BY THEIR CHILDREN,

GRANDCHILDREN, AND FAMILY

Albert Hamway זצ״ל

UNDERSTOOD WHAT JEWISH LIVING

WAS ALL ABOUT.

IN FARAWAY JAPAN HE RAISED HIS CHILDREN

WITH A LOVE FOR THEIR TRADITION.

THEY EACH BUILT

WARM AND LOVING JEWISH HOMES,

PASSING ON TO THEIR CHILDREN AND

THEY TO THEIRS THE FLAME

WHICH THEIR FATHER HAD PASSED TO THEM.

HE IS REMEMBERED WITH LOVE BY

HIS WIFE, HIS CHILDREN,

GRANDCHILDREN,

AND GREAT-GRANDCHILDREN.

מציבים אנו בזה

מזכרת נצח

לאבינו מורנו היקר

ר' לטמן

בן ר' חיים דוב בער ז"ל

איש צנוע

שכל חייו רץ כצבי

לעשות רצון אבינו שבשמים

ולאמנו מורתנו היקרה

רות רבקה לאה

בת ר' אברהם ע"ה

יהא זכרם ברוך

IN LOVING MEMORY

OF

OUR PARENTS

Mollie

AND

Sam E. Levy

*

IN LOVING MEMORY

OF MY BELOVED PARENTS,

AND

MORE, MY GOOD AND PRECIOUS

FRIENDS

Jack & Jeanette Feldman

THEY WERE GENEROUS, WARMHEARTED,

AND GENTLE.

YOU COULD NOT MEET THEM

WITHOUT BEING TOUCHED BY THEIR

GOODNESS.

WITH A SMILE ON HIS WISE FACE

AND NOVHARDOK MUSSAR IN HIS HEART

HaRav Chaim Mordechai Weinkrantz זצ״ל

UNDERSTOOD US ALL SO WELL, SO VERY WELL.

NO PROBLEM,

BUT HIS WISDOM FOUND A SOLUTION.

NO PAIN, BUT HIS EMPATHY

WAS A HEALING BALM.

CHILD OF A CULTURE VERY DIFFERENT

FROM OUR OWN, HE NEVERTHELESS FOUND

COMMONALITY IN HIS AND OUR

JEWISH HEARTS.

WE WILL NEVER FORGET THE BOOKS

WHICH HE SO DILIGENTLY TAUGHT US,

NOR THE LIFE LESSONS

FOR WHICH HE WAS A LIVING TEXT.

—THE MONDAY SHIUR